AUGER

Artist: Francine Auger

Marshall McLuhan, 1911-1980.

Judith Fitzgerald

Award-winning poet, music critic, and literary journalist Judith Fitzgerald began her career in the early 1980s as an Entertainment writer with The *Globe and Mail* (where her work earned the Fiona Mee Literary Journalism Award). Her poetry, reviews, profiles, interviews, criticism, editorials, features, and columns have been published in numerous national and international anthologies, periodicals, journals, and newspapers.

Fitzgerald has published sixteen books of poetry, including *Victory, Rapturous Chronicles, River*, and *Twenty-Six Ways Out of This World*. She has received a Writers' Choice Award and has been shortlisted for the Governor General's Award, the Pat Lowther Award, and the Trillium Award. Fitzgerald's best-selling *Building a Mystery: The Story of Sarah McLachlan and Lilith Fair* (Quarry) was released in December 1997; its update, *Sarah McLachlan: Building a Mystery* (New Millennium Edition: Quarry/ Omnibus), was published in June 2000.

In 1994, with the generous cooperation of the University of Windsor's Assumption College and Department of Communications, Fitzgerald conceived and coordinated *Makin' McLuhan*, a multimedia colloquium the CBC hailed as "an invigorating event which goes a long way towards reclaiming and reaffirming the reputation of one of Canada's foremost thinkers."

In the same collection

Ven Begamudré, *Isaac Brock: Larger Than Life*.
Lynne Bowen, *Robert Dunsmuir: Laird of the Mines*.
Kate Braid, *Emily Carr: Rebel Artist*.
William Chalmers, *George Mercer Dawson: Geologist, Scientist, Explorer*.
Stephen Eaton Hume, *Frederick Banting: Hero, Healer, Artist*.
Naïm Kattan, *A.M. Klein: Poet and Prophet*.
Betty Keller, *Pauline Johnson: First Aboriginal Voice of Canada*.
Michelle Labrèche-Larouche, *Emma Albani: International Star*.
Dave Margoshes, *Tommy Douglas: Building the New Society*.
Raymond Plante, *Jacques Plante: Behind the Mask*.
T.F. Rigelhof, *George Grant: Redefining Canada*.
Arthur Slade, *John Diefenbaker. An Appointment with Destiny*.
John Wilson, *John Franklin: Traveller on Undiscovered Seas*.
John Wilson, *Norman Bethune: A Life of Passionate Conviction*.
Rachel Wyatt, *Agnes Macphail: Champion of the Underdog*.

Marshall McLuhan

Canadian Cataloguing in Publication Data

Fitzgerald, Judith

    Marshall McLuhan : wise guy

    (The Quest Library ; 14).
    Includes bibliographical references and index.

    ISBN 0-9688166-7-3

    1. McLuhan, Marshall, 1911-1980. 2. Mass media specialists – Canada – Biography. I. Title. II. Series: Quest library; 14.

P92.5.M3F57 2001   302.23'092   C200-1941199-5

Legal Deposit: Fourth quarter 2001
National Library of Canada
Bibliothèque nationale du Québec

XYZ Publishing acknowledges the support of The Quest Library project by the Canadian Studies Program and the Book Publishing Industry Development Program (BPIDP) of the Department of Canadian Heritage. The opinions expressed do not necessarily reflect the views of the Government of Canada.

The publishers further acknowledge the financial support our publishing program receives from The Canada Council for the Arts, the ministère de la Culture et des Communications du Québec, and the Société de développement des entreprises culturelles.

Chronology: Judith Fitzgerald
Index: Darcy Dunton
Layout: Édiscript enr.
Cover design: Zirval Design
Cover illustration: Francine Auger
Photo research: Cynthia Cecil
Editorial assistant: Cheryl Taylor

Printed and bound in Canada

XYZ Publishing
1781 Saint Hubert Street
Montreal, Quebec   H2L 3Z1
Tel: (514) 525-2170
Fax: (514) 525-7537
E-mail: xyzed@mlink.net
Web site: www.xyzedit.com

Distributed by:
General Distribution Services
325 Humber College Boulevard
Toronto, Ontario   M9W 7C3
Tel: (416) 213-1919
Fax: (416) 213-1917
E-mail: cservice@genpub.com

JUDITH FITZGERALD

MCLUHAN

Marshall

WISE GUY

Publishing

Acknowledgments

To Philip Marchand, whose McLuhaniacal investigations always inspire my own, thank you for your coyote generosity and, especially, for making a difference: The template is perfect; the errors are mine. I shall always remain deeply grateful for your willingness to share your brilliant work and research as a collaborator *in absentia* in the making of *Marshall McLuhan: Wise Guy.*

To XYZ's editorial director, Rhonda Bailey, mere thanks cannot begin to express my admiration and respect for your good sense and great spirit. You make the editorial process a genuine pleasure. *Marshall McLuhan: Wise Guy* is *our* labour of love.

To Peter C. Newman, Canadian National Arguranter Extraordinaire, heartfelt thanks for your generosity and support of *Marshall McLuhan: Wise Guy* and the Quest Library biography series.

To Daniel "DTM" Jalowica, muchical boundlinesses for your invaluable input and overall irreplaceability.

To Connie & Paul McKenna, André Vanasse, Dick & Lenore Langs, T. F. Rigelhof, Francine Auger,

Cheryl Taylor, Darcy Dunton, and Cynthia Cecil, a round of heartfelt thanks.

To Kelley Lynch & Lennie C., Leon, Musia, Susan & Robert Schwartz, and Marie Mazur (thank you for rhythm, reason, and rhyme).

To Carol McIntyre, Helen Major, and Wayne Snow at the Sundridge Post Office (thank you for all the neat treats and feats).

Special thanks to Irving Layton, Assumption University's President Father Bill Irwin, David Sobelman, Monique Pasternak, Adam & Martin Levin, Joan Ramsay, Dafydd Price Jones, Michael S. Connaghan, Taku Moero, Robert Parkins, Anne Marie Smart/Parkins, Laurie Smith, Mark Barker, and Antonio D'Alfonso.

To Henry Blanco, Library Assistant in the Archives and Special Collections of the A. C. Long Health Sciences Library at Columbia University, thank you for the invaluable additional information you graciously provided for the "Wise Guy to the World" chapter.

To the Writers' Union of Canada, the Canada Council, the Public Lending Rights Commission, CanCopy, and the Ontario Arts Council, thank you for your continued support. Without your assistance, *Marshall McLuhan: Wise Guy* would not exist.

The medium, or process, of our time – electric technology – is reshaping and restructuring patterns of social interdependence and every aspect of our personal life. It is forcing us to reconsider and re-evaluate practically every thought, every action, and every institution formerly taken for granted. Everything is changing – you, your family, your neighbourhood, your education, your job, your government, your relation to "the others." And they're changing dramatically.
– Marshall McLuhan
and Quentin Fiore,
The Medium Is the Massage (1967)

To Philip Marchand, Michelle & Monica McKenna, Isaac Gray, Donna, Geoff, April, Sarah & Laura Gompers, and Valerie, Ruth & Leah Shertzman.

Contents

Introduction

Critical Mass

The better part of my work on media is actually somewhat like a safe-cracker's. I don't know what's inside; maybe it's nothing. I just sit down and start to work. I grope, I listen, I test, I accept and discard; I try out different sequences – until the tumblers fall and the doors spring open.

– Marshall McLuhan

What Sigmund Freud is to psychoanalysis, Dr. Herbert Marshall McLuhan (1911-1980) is to communication theory and cultural anthropology. One of the most influential intellectual mavericks of twentieth-century thought, McLuhan began his career working within the relatively obscure confines of the ivory tower where he toiled away polishing essays analyzing literature and creating lectures on how to appreciate its merits and values.

Stylization, not imitation, was the key to McLuhan's approach. His speciality was media and he simply overturned all assumptions concerning same: "All media are active metaphors in their power to translate experience into new forms. The spoken word was the first technology by which man was able to let go of his environment in order to grasp it in a new way," he explained in *Understanding Media: The Extensions of Man* (1964).

Something of a seer-savant, most likely a genius (but most assuredly a giant on our cultural landscape), Canada's best-known visionary imagined the future and mapped its contours in living colour. Now, his magical and initially bewildering signature, "the medium is the message," seamlessly supports his reputation as a "crisis" philosopher on the razor's edge of the information revolution. More than any other single individual, McLuhan equipped the planet's current population with the mental charts, graphs, maps, and practical means to learn its way through the maze of what he termed The Age of Information.

Through his groundbreaking explorations, investigations, and "probes" (he believed a thinking person must poke and prod everything from language to reality to self-identity), McLuhan developed tools to respond to the overwhelming technological challenges that confront the information-glutted "contemporary anybodies" sleepwalking through life's miraculous vistas (through no fault of their own).

A humanist to the core, McLuhan discerned that the post-industrial world derives its unity from technological imperatives and corporate or political forces rather than from nature, social responsibilities, or human-scale requirements. Investigation of the electr(on)ic world's media and methods has replaced philosophical inquiry into worlds both natural and mechanical. The media of communication in the age of information have replaced the means of production, the overriding system of the era of industrialization. Now, of course, it's clear the world's in the midst of a revolution – a breakup, breakdown, breakthrough – from the age of industry (where the means dominated) to the age of information (where the media dominate).

Taking his cue from author and painter Wyndham Lewis's observation that the "present cannot be revealed to people until it has become yesterday," McLuhan points out individuals see only the past as part and parcel of what he termed "the rear-view mirror phenomenon" obscuring the present and obliterating the future.

According to McLuhan, each new medium produces a new cultural environment that becomes invisible while making visible the one of the previous culture. Enter the artist, the only figure capable of apprehending what will happen since artists naturally see what is happening (or, by definition, they are not artists). The artist is a uniquely capable translator of the "invisible" cultural environment of the present.

Doffing his thinking cap to poet Robert Browning's "The Faultless Painter" as well as novelist James Joyce's zest for the palimpsest (an aphoristic phrase resonating with echoes of its genesis in a source outside itself), the incorrigible neologizer shamelessly promoted his agenda in one of his funniest – punniest? – messages:

"A man's reach must exceed his grasp or what's a metaphor?"

Believing "we become what we behold," McLuhan went further: "We shape our tools and they in turn shape us." In all his work, in fact, it's not too far-fetched to suggest McLuhan penned a mournful eulogy for the billions of individuals (contemporary anybodies) afflicted with what he called "psychic rigor mortis," that state where the human being is stripped of personal identity, conscripted into uniform conformity, and thwarted from truly living and experiencing a full and fruitful life by the unrelenting demands media, corporate, and commercial interests make upon any and all who hang around what he termed the global village.

The substance of his work and the style of his writing are considered to be apocalyptic, inscrutable, dogmatic, contradictory, bereft of traditional modes of scholarly or critical methodology, and dismissive of careful and close argumentation in favour of repetition, paradox, and dizzying digression. In response, McLuhan defends his collage-like approach as the only one capable of fully conveying the chaos, complexity, and contradictions of contemporary life. Breakdown inevitably leads to breakthrough, which always yields to greater understanding and the fine art of meaningful communication.

An advocate of simultaneous perception (global thinking) from the moment he first discovered its benefits during his studies of New Criticism at Cambridge, Professor McLuhan subsequently adopted the view that the only way to approach a work of literature was to examine it in terms of the way it works its magic or achieves its effects (rather than focusing exclusively on its major themes, representative motifs, or the biography of its creator).

McLuhan intuitively understood that television signalled a threat to literacy and that computers would rapidly become extensions of the human being's central nervous system by expanding its range of sense perceptions. In the 1960s, when the relatively new medium of television was radical, instant, and global, McLuhan was frequently mentioned on Rowan and Martin's hip comedy programme, *Laugh-In*. At the same time, the metaphysician of media was informing GE, Bell Telephone, and IBM they were not in the business of light bulbs, telephones, and business machines; rather, they were in the business of moving information. *The medium is the message*. In 1980, the year McLuhan met his Maker, CNN was up and running while personal computers were quickly becoming affordable acquisitions throughout the Western world.

"McLuhan," literary critic Northrop Frye astutely observed in 1988, "was celebrated for the wrong reasons in the 1960s, and then neglected for the wrong reasons later." Frye called for a long overdue reassessment of McLuhan's work and its value. Four years later, a *Mondo 2000* scribe marvelled that "reading McLuhan is like reading Shakespeare – you keep stumbling on phrases that you thought were clichés, only this guy made them up!"

The name is McLuhan, Marshall McLuhan. *The Oxford English Dictionary (OED)* lists it in 346 entries, one of which cites Quentin Fiore, the gifted artist-designer who teamed up with McLuhan to create *The Medium Is the Massage*, the 1967 bestseller featuring playful and exhilarating spins, swirls, comminglings, and intertwinglings of texts, images, and graphics that, thirty-odd years later, would come to serve as the template for magazines such as *Shift*, *Details*, and *Wired*.

Most importantly, though, McLuhan's observations have since come into their own as profound commentaries on the ways in which relationships among individuals have been altered in Cyberia, where the body remains parked (or paralyzed) while the mind of the techno-traveller jacks in and roams the gratification grids of the information galaxy.

As with many of McLuhan's pronouncements (including those that seem to have divined the nature and dynamics of the Internet many years before it even existed), this one seems to have been made by one of those unique individuals capable of peering into the future. A number of his observations baffled and astonished audiences at the time – the outrageousness of some of them tempted his apoplectic critics to describe his theories as "McLuhanacy." Now, in the first decade of the new millennium, they seem perfectly intelligible.

It's no surprise the prophet designation was – and continues to be – bandied about by many who search for a word to adequately describe the impact of insights and "outerings" (utterances) that boggle most minds. In his examination of the individual in the context of the global via the national, McLuhan correctly perceived electronic media would annihilate local culture. In the neo-tribalist global village where personality has been erased, sex sells and violence erupts as a quest for identity writ graphic.

As McLuhan astutely observed, new technologies would extend the range of both body and mind in ways that irrevocably altered an individual's relationships with both the environment and every other resident of the global village, creating a universal nervous system of vast complexity and sophistication shared by any and all in possession of the inclination and the equipment to participate.

Since the modern world seems now to have achieved that "complete break with five-thousand years of mechanical technology" McLuhan identifies as his "main theme," the "outerings" of the human sensorium (the senses considered collectively) combine and recombine to produce what he called *network consciousness* and what individuals have come to recognize as the realization of his "percept" that human beings will experience a world where the illusion of depth proliferates and all-inclusive nowness reaches critical mass.

Not surprisingly, then, when one of McLuhan's friends asked him whether he really believed there was life after death, McLuhan cagily answered the question with one of his own:

"Do you really believe there is any life before death?"

Judith Fitzgerald
Canada Day 2001
The Beautiful Downtown Middle of Nowhere

His mother knows he is
"destined for greatness right around the globe."
Elsie and Herbert Marshall McLuhan.

1

Lasting Impressions

Radio was inseparable from the rise of jazz culture as TV has been inseparable from the rise of
rock culture.

— Marshall McLuhan

Across the river, the lanky boy, all spindleshanked
and elbows akimbo, sees the clearing below the
massive maple where he and Red built that disaster of
a tree fort, that rather ram-shackly effort that collapsed
when the winds from the north blustered through
Winnipeg last fall. He finds the view restful, calming,
an antidote to the rages, knots, and tangles of angry
voices ricocheting around the walls back at the house.
The Assiniboine flows peacefully, predictably, snaking

gracefully into the haze of the sun's brilliant afternoon light further upstream, right next to where the boat he's building with Red is cradled on its sawhorses in Mr. Levin's garage.

Mars dreams the boat's finished and he and Red are rowing together, steering the little vessel into the future, away from the insanity, arguments, and hysterical catastrophes back at the house. *No doubt*, thinks he, remembering his only brother, *Red's cowering beneath the back stairs, quietly crying, per usual.* Red doesn't mind the noise the way his older brother minds it. Mars minds it terribly; the shrieks and screechings rip his guts out. *Red's got more tolerance. He's got a much better attitude about all of it.*

As for Mars? He hates it. He simply hates it. Why can't people just get along, be happy with each other, understand that nobody's perfect (or everybody is, since that's God's will)? If everybody *were* perfect, why, we'd bore each other to death, sighs he, audibly perplexed, kicking the root of the elm exposed by the river's erosion.

Well, even though he's only nine, he reasons, he's not too young to promise himself he'll marry an agreeable woman, a peace-loving woman who doesn't have to scream and yell and pick fights to make her points, an order-craving woman who understands the meaning of "compromise." Someone with sparkling eyes, a sweet smile, and a forgiving nature, someone who doesn't have to be right 100 per cent of the time. Yep. That's the best he can do. Swear he'll never marry a screamer. *Sheesh.*

By the time Mars reaches the garage, he's already feeling a little better. A lark perches on the roof, laughingly hopping from foot to foot, happily mocking the long-faced kid. Mars examines the tiny bird closely, thinking it's not a big fancy thing but – it's up there on the roof of the Levins' garage strutting and mimicking Mars to beat the band. Sassy little devil. Sort of like the boat he's building with Red. *It'll float*, thinks Mars, squaring his lantern jaw. *It'll float*. He'll make it float. All the doubters will eat their words. If he has to bail water till the cows keel over, that boat will float.

The lark on the Levins' roof, perfectly on cue, whistles in affirmation. Mars swears it. And, that's what he'll call the boat, too. *The Lark*. For a lark on the river with Red in the boat that will most definitely float.

Count on it.

Almost a decade into the twentieth century, highly intelligent and ambitious nineteen-year-old Elsie Naomi Hall, in possession of a freshly minted teacher's certificate from Acadia, Nova Scotia's then-Baptist university, joins her family in Mannville, Alberta; within weeks, she's handily secured a position in one of the area's better schools. It is there, at a Sunday picnic, the delicate and doe-eyed beauty proudly announces she's met and plans to marry the tall, handsome, and charming Herbert McLuhan on 31 December 1909.

A year later, the adventurous newlyweds relocate a hundred miles due west to Edmonton to begin their life together. While the amiable Herb forms a promising real-estate company –McLuhan, Sullivan & McDonald – with his trio of partners, Elsie prepares for the 21 July 1911 arrival of the first of their two sons, Herbert Marshall, just before the couple takes up permanent residence in their spacious two-storey custombuilt home in Edmonton's well-to-do Highlands district. Then, following the birth of Marshall's younger brother, Maurice Raymond, on 9 August 1913 (and the addition of Rags, the family's beloved Airedale collie), Elsie declares the clan complete.

On 28 June 1914, as tensions escalate in the Balkans, an assassin's bullet fells Austria-Hungary's heir to the Hapsburg throne, Archduke Ferdinand, in Sarajevo, signalling the symbolic beginning of the First World War.

Herb enlists. He gallantly insists Elsie and the boys return to her family in Middleton, Nova Scotia, near the Bay of Fundy; but, for reasons of either flu or flat feet, Herb's army days are numbered. Instead of returning to Edmonton, however, the couple reasons the family will probably fare better in the flourishing railroad city of Winnipeg, Manitoba, the financial capital of Canada's West (as well as the home of the Alice Leone Mitchell School of Expression where Elsie elects to pursue her elocutionary studies and hone her oratorical skills training in the "principles of public reading" and dramatic performance).

Herb enters the life-insurance business (and is soon demoted from manager to salesman); Elsie becomes the School of Expression's top student. In 1921, the McLuhans finally settle into a suitable rental dwelling among the Scots and Irish in Winnipeg's Fort-Rouge residential district.

∞

Marshall – "Mars" to his copper-topped brother, Maurice ("Red"); "Marsh" or "Mac" to everyone else – is hurting. Elsie's disciplined him yet again with the razor strop. Maurice knows the feeling; but, if he doesn't mind his Ps and Qs, Marshall could well turn on him; so, he keeps his mouth shut and makes himself as inconspicuous as possible. For a minute or two. Then, well, Maurice being Maurice (and almost eight years old), he tries to make the best of things.

"Mars? Marsy?"

"Yeah? What, Red?"

"Are you okay?"

"I'll live. Don't worry. I'll live."

"Mars?"

"Yeah, Red?"

"Do you want me to help you work on *The Lark* tomorrow?"

"No, I don't think so, not tomorrow."

"Okay, Mars. Okay."

"Maybe on Sunday, though?"

"Really?"

"Sure. Right after Sunday school. Okay, Red?"

"Okay."

"Yeah, it's okay, Red, it's really okay. See? Nothing's broken."

∞

Through the most wonderful as well as the worst years of their young lives, the curious and adventurous

McLuhan boys enjoy (or endure) an up-and-down existence in the lively McLuhan household at 507 Gertrude Avenue, passing the days hiking with Herb, looking up and memorizing difficult words in the dictionary, skiing in winter and, during the languid summer hiatus, carousing on the banks of the Assiniboine at one end of Gertrude or swimming in the Red at the other; but, once Mars finishes building *The Lark*, the inseparable pair spends long hours sailing and rowing on both rivers.

∞

As highly motivated as Elsie is (and Herb is not), the boys' mother strives to improve her family's fortunes and offers elocution lessons, a not-uncommon practice at the time. In the years following the First World War, prior to the proliferation of radio, youngsters regularly study public-speaking and dramatic recitation.

Pupils flock to the house on Gertrude, eager to learn proper breathing, enunciation, memorization, articulation, and performance techniques. Elsie doesn't provide her sons with formal training in elocution, but both pick up plenty by osmosis and remain excellent speakers for the duration (despite Maurice's feeling he spent much of his early life trying to keep up with his brother).

Maurice, who speaks frequently to church groups, will grow up to become a man of the cloth for several years (before committing himself to the teaching profession). His older brother will grow up to become a man on a mission with a message concerning media in the future, in some far-off time and unimaginable place all will come to call the global village.

⌒

Glimmers of McLuhan's love of devices and machines capable of transmitting words, music, and messages surface. One of the biggest thrills of his adolescent years, in fact, is fiddling with gadgets and such, especially new-fangled gadgets that allow him to tune into the world of radio late at night, picking up stations from as far away as Pittsburgh, Pennsylvania, hundreds of miles southeast of the Manitoba border.

Pittsburgh's out there, a vibrant metropolis in a huge world just waiting to be investigated, a world filled with wonders as plentiful as stars, a huge and noisy world far beyond Gertrude Avenue except when – with the cooperation of the northern lights – the reception is brilliant and Pittsburgh's KDKA comes through clean, clear, and wholly spellbinding.

McLuhan spends his after-school hours attending classes to earn his crystal-set operator's licence. To celebrate his success, he builds a state-of-the-art radio with double sets of earplugs so both he and Red can listen to KDKA before they drift off to sleep but, naturally, not before Mars and Red trade facts they'd studied at school that day:

"The telegraph, invented in 1844, transmits information at five bits per second."

"Oh, yeah? Poet John Milton lost his eyesight in February 1652, most likely because of glaucoma."

"*Pfft!* Because of heavy traffic congestion, Julius Caesar banned all wheeled vehicles from Rome during daylight hours...."

Facts, figures, fictions, flights of fancy. Throughout these impressionable years, McLuhan despairs of ever learning everything he believes he really needs to know. He studies long hours and spends countless more memorizing long passages of poetry and dramatic prose.

Elsie, similarly motivated (but more concerned with method, performance, and delivery), even practises Browning poems and Shakespearean sonnets in tones both spirited and mesmerizing while doing the housework, running the carpet-sweeper over the Persian rug she's finally acquired or replacing the slab of ice in the bottom tray of the brand-new icebox she's recently purchased.

By the time McLuhan enters university, he's read, heard, memorized, and consumed almost everything of value and interest written in the English language with the notable exception of *Paradise Lost*, John Milton's epic poem. (He considers it beyond his comprehension at his inexperienced age.) In his zeal to "own literature," McLuhan handily (if not unconsciously) prepares himself for the very (ivory) towers (of Babel) he'll eventually topple. After all, he's strangely convinced he's on his way to becoming the man with the message for the human race poised, then, as now, on the brink of one complicated yet potentially beautiful new world.

∞

McLuhan's immediate world, once he comes to understand it better, begins to reveal its own set of complications. For one thing, his parents, slowly drifting apart as his mother's on-stage ventures take off and his father's career never does, quarrel fiercely, frequently, all too often forgetting the stress and anguish they're rather selfishly inflicting upon their captive audience.

Elsie is extremely ambitious; Herb is not. Elsie wants to beautify the Gertrude Street dwelling; Herb is content to live within its walls exactly as it is. Elsie wants to be the first on the block to own a car; Herb never owns one in his life. The stylish Elsie is, in short, a *woman*; the casual Herb, as she tells the boys in mean-spirited disgust for her husband's disinterest in all things fashionable, is not a *man*.

Herb, a maddeningly mild-mannered and agreeable man, is happy to sit back and shoot the breeze. He loves his sons very much and spends long hours with them, delighting in their intellectual progress and generally staying out of harm's way. One game the trio particularly enjoys involves finding, learning, and memorizing the meanings of the most difficult words in the dictionary, a daily habit his firstborn, now a self-described "intellectual thug," adopts for life.

Despite the fact Maurice is more his father's top banana and strong-willed Marshall tends to be the apple of Elsie's eye, the boys are close, probably because their mother's "boundless egotism," as her eldest describes it, requires they stick together for protection during her emotional storms.

Privately, McLuhan bemoans the cruel fate that has brought his parents together as both he and Red witness the frenzied events that will ultimately tear the ill-suited couple apart. Then, not suprisingly, when Elsie blows her stack for no good reason either child sees, her sons become easy targets for her fury and frustration.

Later, McLuhan observes his childhood was so very painful in some respects that he can barely stand to think about it. Yet, he loves and respects his mother, somehow intuitively grasping the psychological dynamic fuelling her ballistics derives from her own childhood, damaged by an intense, unpredictable, and volatile taskmaster of a father given to temper tantrums of legendary status among locals.

Naturally, when the often-generous (and certainly incomparable) Elsie brags about either the talented Maurice or the gifted Marshall to the many people she invites to break bread at the family's table – lavishly praising their brilliant minds, excellent behaviour, and strapping young physiques – both boys glow with pride.

∞

McLuhan fails grade six. His schoolteacher mother, well-acquainted with her son's intellectual abilities, naturally sets the principal straight concerning the school's problem. Her son, a brilliant young genius, truly destined for greatness, is simply bored, bored, BORED. When McLuhan enters grade seven on the condition he "handle it," he handles it, thanks to a teacher who loves words, language, and literature as much as he does.

It is during this pivotal year that McLuhan finally discovers the path he believes he must tread; and, later, by the time he's making inroads at the University of Manitoba in 1928, he's already proven his mother right.

⌒

McLuhan can see lovely splashes of stars, sparkling jewels so close and bright, clear nights in the fragrant garden on Gertrude; yes, he can see the splendid stars, he can almost scoop up handfuls of them; and, yes, one day – whether he becomes an engineer, doctor, or Olympic rower – he will see the name of Marshall McLuhan glittering magnificently among them, no doubt because he's finally figured out what it is he wants to do.

He enters the University of Manitoba fully convinced his interest in structure and design will be put to best use studying engineering, but after spending that summer working among a crew of surveyors in the wilds of mosquito-friendly Manitoba, McLuhan anguishes over his future before switching to English and philosophy, a decision that proves to be one of the best he makes.

Nonetheless, the young scholar's tormented by feelings of inadequacy and his fear that, although he now knows what he wants to study, he's still no closer to determining how he'll realize his dream of becoming a Great Man once his studying days are done.

A Christian who reads the Bible daily, McLuhan had attended Winnipeg's Nassau Baptist Church (at his mother's insistence), even though his father was

Presbyterian; as he matured, McLuhan opted to attend any Church but the dull and stuffy Baptist one. One breezy evening in April 1930, sitting on the throne and pondering what he'd just learned in Sunday school that day, it comes to him:

He'll write a Great Book that will prove all life – mental, material, spiritual, physical – is governed by laws, laws that no one else has even noticed, laws that no else has even considered discussing between the covers of a book. *His* book will be philosophically grounded in this world; it will not be a religious book; but, its central idea, issuing from Christ's precepts and McLuhan's understanding of the primary importance of Pentecost in view of the laws he's perceived, will provide comfort and enlightenment. The laws are infallible – as precise as mathematics, as ubiquitous as weather – and, if a person correctly grasps them in all their glory, a person goes a long way.

Pentecost is the divine mystery, the all-encompassing power or energy responsible for the miracle of creation.

Thus, because the world exists – living beings see, feel, hear, taste, touch, smell, and know it – the human race owes allegiance to it (or, more accurately, to its Creator and the fruits of His labour). In believing in Pentecost as the divine mystery, McLuhan pledges his own allegiance to the philosophy of Saint Thomas Aquinas (1226-1274), the theologian canonized as the patron saint of students and universities in 1323 as well as one of the greatest and most influential religious thinkers (who had, incidentally, taken a vow of chastity and renounced the trappings of this world).

Saint Thomas wrote numerous lucid and erudite volumes (including the *Summa Theologica*), and he also preached with great eloquence and inspiring conviction concerning his certainty God exists and His proof is everywhere (in everything) in this world in which we live. Throughout his life McLuhan will maintain close ties with the so-called Thomist School. His idea of the "sensuously orchestrated" individual of the future corresponds with doctrines aligning God with universal laws and forces; but, as a self-described Thomist, his philosophical position maintains existence is the supreme perfection – being in God and creation – while human knowledge is acquired through sense experience which leads to reflective activity. He often quips, "Should Old Aquinas be forgot," when he's queried about his faith, thus demonstrating his willingness to show his true Thomistic colours.

The colourful McLuhan comes to believe that "all the university taught you to do was bullshit." Still, he's anxious to discuss his revealing insights and fresh ideas with fellow student and kindred spirit, Tom Easterbrook. Tom and Marsh, the best of buddies, argue incessantly, sparring over virtually everything, some nights roaming the streets well into the wee hours, when the rising sun reminds them a little shut-eye might not be such a bad idea.

It is during these heady months the young thinker decides he needs to address both his weight and love life (or, more precisely, his skinniness and love lack). McLuhan stands six-foot-one-and-a-quarter inches or 1.86 metres tall and tips the scales at a little under 140 pounds or 63.5 kilograms. He takes up scrumming on rugby fields, skirmishing in makeshift hockey rinks, distance swimming at the YMCA and, even though some of his classmates consider the debate-loving brainiac a "moron," he thoroughly enjoys dancing at university affairs and socials.

Apparently, the striking young man in possession of a certain wayward charm cuts quite the elegant figure on the dance floor, especially when the tuneful tenor stylings of Vaudevillian Harry Lauder float dreamily through the highly charged air.

∞

Just after jotting a few self-defining thoughts in his journal concerning the way in which his bookishness and elevated sexual ideals all but preclude the possibility that he, Marshall McLuhan, will be foolish enough to fall in love before he turns thirty and is better equipped to select a suitable wife for someone such as himself – a gentle, wholesome, and sympathetic woman who will balance, tame, and make him whole – McLuhan does, in fact, fall madly, crazily, passionately in love. He tumbles head-over-heartstrings for Marjorie Norris, a lissom medical student possessed of incomparable beauty, sterling character, and a superior intellect (not to mention her generally soothing and sunny disposition).

∞

Drats! She already has a boyfriend, a steady-as-Freddie beau? What's that you say? His name is Jimmy Munroe? Rats, drats, and double-drats! I beg your pardon? Really? No! Well, now, what's the latest item of interest making the rounds of the university grapevine? A rumour? Could it be true?

YES! It's true! Marjorie ditched the dasher! No! She says she wouldn't mind a date with young Marshall! She'd simply be delighted, in fact. Delighted! *She'd simply be delighted...* Who'd a-thunk it? Marjorie Norris? Ha! There is a God!

∞

The full moon floats just above the horizon, luminous and huge, one fine evening in April on the banks of the Assiniboine. She sits prettily on a tree stump. He stands contentedly beside her. All is right with the world.

"Have you ever seen such a moon, bathed in the most fragile strands of clouds, just whispered hints of mistiness, almost a shimmering halo? It's beautiful, Marjorie, isn't it?"

"It is when you describe it, Marshall."

"If I kissed you, do you think you'd see the after-image of the moon when you closed your eyes?"

"I'm not sure... why? Do you think you would like to experiment?"

"Well... If you didn't think I was being too forward."

"Oh, Marshall, I wouldn't think that. This would be an experiment, after all, wouldn't it?"

"Well... Yes, it would; it is, too. It's exactly that... An experiment! You see, Mademoiselle, I've never kissed a girl before..."

∽

Prior to the University of Manitoba's acceptance of his master's thesis in 1934, McLuhan discovers with bemusement he has indeed become an integral element in the general mix of faculty and students on campus. During his years in its Department of English, he'd penned several brilliant and occasionally controversial articles for the student paper, *The Manitoban*.

In "Tomorrow and Tomorrow," for example, he'd illuminated various aspects of corruption he'd identified in the fabric of his society and culture. Detractors charged him with ultra-conservatism and holier-than-thou tendencies, ignoring the possibility an individual can truly believe in an older and better time, a time when the human race wasn't going through the mechanical motions in a punch-the-clock universe. Many of history's finest writers – from Chaucer, Shakespeare, and Dickens to Eliot, Joyce, and Blake – have similarly expressed righteous wrath regarding the abhorrent and dehumanizing effects of methods not unlike those McLuhan decried.

R. C. Lodge – one professor who has the pleasure of witnessing McLuhan in action when he teaches him at the University – remembers the exceptional elocutionist who also came to be an excellent sailor as "the most outstanding student" he's known.

With endorsements of that calibre supporting his application, the up-and-coming go-getter's awarded the sixteen-hundred-dollar Imperial Order of the Daughters of the Empire Scholarship. McLuhan's mother urges him to apply to Boston's Harvard University. He gently urges her to mind her own business. He'll make his own plans, especially after last summer (when Easterbrook and McLuhan had worked their way across the ocean to spend several months bumming around the UK).

In plain English, the determined young scholar will most certainly pursue his studies (either at Oxford or at Cambridge). That's definitely that. There's nothing to discuss. There's absolutely no chance he'll change his mind. Nope. Never. Not in this life.

For once, Elsie butts out.

McLuhan decides upon Cambridge after he fails in his pursuit of a Rhodes' Scholarship because, during the crucial oral-examination of the applicant for that honour, the erudite and outspoken petitioner gets into hot water when the none-too-wise guy refuses to back-paddle on a point he considers worthy of heated debate with one of the examiners.

"Mr. McLooklin, are we to believe you are seriously suggesting the study of comic books is a worthy enterprise and pursuit for scholarly young minds? We? The sages of Oxford upon whom your clearly sad and sorry fate so tenuously rests? WE are to believe this utter nonsense, Mr. McLockland?"

"Excuse me, it's McLuhan, Sir. Marshall McLuhan? Herbert Marshall McLuhan? That's *moi*. Muck – Loo – Ann – McLuhan! And, yup, I am fully prepared to have you believe with all your heart and soul the study of comic books is a serious enterprise for young scholars looking fruitfully at our world as it exists right now, at this very moment, if you get my drift. Surely you can't deny that comic books comprise an essential element of contemporary culture and there-fore warrant investigation as cultural artefacts, if noth-ing else? *Ka-zam! Ka-bam! Wowie ka-zowie!*"

∽

The committee, naturally, instantly nixes any notion Mr. McLuhan may have nurtured concerning his atten-dance at Oxford, a respectable and respected institu-tion where students respect their betters (instead of besting them in dogged intellectual argumentation).

∽

No matter. Cambridge has better professors anyway *plus*, he's already been accepted by that respected institution *plus*, his fave aunt's already lent him the additional funds necessary for his English education *plus*, Marjorie will continue her medical studies while waiting for him *plus*, once Dr. McLuhan returns from overseas and Dr. McLuhan realizes her dream of opening a practice in the bustling heart of downtown Winnipeg, the pair will tie the proverbial knot.

In other words, it all adds up.

McLuhan's placidity belies the tumult of ideas swirling
in his brain during his Cambridge days.

2

First Comes Love,
Then Comes Cambridge

> The *OED* is Western scholarship's greatest
> achievement.
>
> – Marshall McLuhan

O n top of his game, fresh from Winnipeg, flush
with funds (despite the general dearth of same
among the population due to the Great Depression),
head very much in love's lofty clouds, McLuhan hits
bottom at Cambridge with an abrupt and rather humil-
iating *ka-thunk*. "One advantage we Westerners have is
that we're under no illusion we've had an education,"
McLuhan later muses concerning his rude awakening

at the progressive university best described as Genius Central. "That's why I started at the bottom again," he adds, fully believing his provincial Canadian education means nothing more than the fact he's back at square diddly-zip.

Such is the response to the advanced state of study and reading in his newest endeavours in the English canon under the direction and tutelage of literary luminaries the quality of I. A. Richards (*Principles of Literary Criticism*, 1924; *Practical Criticism*, 1929), F. R. Leavis (*Mass Civilisation and Minority Culture*, 1930; *New Bearings in English Poetry*, 1932; *Culture and Environment*, co-authored with Denys Thompson, 1933); and, Q. D. Leavis (*Fiction and the Reading Public*, 1932).

But, right now, it's October 1934 in England and it's gloriously bracing. Crisp and sparkling days yield to sunsets embroidered with silvery hints of rose and aqua signalling the arrival of that famous British chill spell. Night descends, the nocturnal velvet blueness restorative and soothing. McLuhan ranges over narrow gas-lit streets or takes his time over tea in one of the many shops wholly devoted to the country's revered cuppa. He loves the night, the muffled quiet, the comforting shadows of the hearth's flames licking the walls in his spacious room; indeed, throughout his life, he will find nothing more soothing than sitting by a well-tended fire, recalling his favourite easy chair on Cambridge's Magrath Avenue, fondly remembering eating, drinking, and later, either smoking a fine cigar or stoking and restoking his favourite pipe. (McLuhan, incidentally, smokes his first cigarette in May 1935; in December of that year, he becomes slightly inebriated for the first time.)

The ambience invigorates the hicksical Canuck outsider who's come to Cambridge's Trinity Hall driven by the dream of securing a very impressive M. Litt. or Ph.D. in his advanced studies of the English language and its finest literature. After living in near-poverty in Winnipeg with his father, McLuhan promises himself he'll become prominent doing some sort of extraordinary work. He'll never again lack for sufficient funds. And, once he settles into his new life in the large and lovely room with its wonderful fireplace, he knows he's one giant step closer to keeping the vow he made.

Undaunted by what others think of his not-so-proper credentials, already well-practised in the art of dismissing those who ridicule him as proof of nothing but their own ridiculosities, McLuhan tears into his studies with all the ferocity of a wanderer in the desert dying of starvation and thirst suddenly realizing the oasis into which he's stumbled is anything but a mirage.

It most certainly is not a mirage. Nor are McLuhan's years at Cambridge a disappointment. Anything but. The experience opens his eyes, ears, and mind to near-limitless possibilities, confirming for him his feeling that, if he is indeed going to make his mark on this rapidly changing world, there is no better way to go about doing so than by immersing himself in the stimulating intellectual culture so abundantly available in this refuge from the wild and crazy world beyond its borders. Look no further than the fact that Elsie has left Herbert, has taken Red to go off and make her way in Toronto's theatre world and – almost unbelievably –

the pair's now living in a roominghouse on Selby Street, in the very heart of Cabbagetown, in the city's working-class neighbourhood. Go figure, eh?

∞

Happily, at Cambridge, McLuhan flourishes. The world-renowned university is credited with reinventing and revitalizing literary criticism through its pioneering efforts to bring it into the twentieth century (from the morass of the nineteenth century's high romanticism and peculiar standards). Lionel Elvin, McLuhan's tutor, comments that when the twenty-three-year-old consults with him, he finds him willing, open, amiable, intense, and earnest; he's not, however, earnest in any plodding nor sycophantic sense of that word; in fact, he still has a playful light in his eye; and, of necessity, he still continues to hold himself and his ideas in healthy esteem.

Naturally, McLuhan begins to take his health more seriously; in order to achieve his goals at Cambridge, he'd logically reasoned, he'll need to stay in tip-top mental and physical shape; thus, when he learns the Trinity Hall boat club's training new crewmen, he goes along to the trials and secures a place as oarsman with one of the crews.

McLuhan considers it an honour to wear his team's heavy white Trinity Hall sweater; and, when he bulks up to 151 pounds or 68 kg, he notes with satisfaction his training diet – lots of fish and meat (preferably mutton or beef steak), veggies, eggs, toast, and fruit, all topped off with a pint of beer – is working its magic.

During his second year, McLuhan relocates to rooms at Trinity Hall; once settled, he surveys his pleasing domain and thinks, *How lovely this all is, how fortunate I am. Truly, this is happiness. My love of life has never been greater.* And, although the rower's team is never the fastest, it does sufficiently well in one race – placing fifth – that its members are rewarded with the oars they'd only been allowed to borrow until that achievement. It means a great deal to McLuhan, evidenced in the fact his Cambridge oar is always given pride of place in every office he occupies throughout his life.

In 1910, Cambridge had created the King Edward VII Professorship of English Literature, a position towards which the greatest literary theorists of the new century had naturally gravitated; thus, fortuitously, McLuhan's greatest mentors, the ones who most affected his own course in life – not to mention his approaches to literature, culture, technology, and theory – are, among others, Professors I. A. Richards and F. R. Leavis, now universally recognized as two of the granddaddies of what came to be called the New Criticism.

Extremely influential as a school of formal investigation into literature, New Criticism's principles rest upon the belief the author of a given work is not as important as that author's creation. The creation exists independent of the author who created it; it exists for its own sake; and, it contains its own logic and justification which have nothing to do with its creator's life, intent, history, or biography. A New Critic doesn't snoop into the details of the private life of the author, in other words, a New Critic examines the author's creation and aids readers in their appreciation of the work's form, technique, and effects (based upon the belief that all worthy and valuable Western literature is part of a great tradition rooted in ancient Greece). New Criticism emphasizes formal considerations alongside techniques that achieve their desired effects upon readers. Context and relationship within a given work of art are as important as form and content; additionally, the New Critic endorses this tradition of excellence, the so-called Western Canon, and points out ways a given work of art supports and reinforces the valuable in literature (worthy of study for edification or enlightenment) based upon the principles clearly on display in the great works of the Western Canon.

New Criticism provides the key and unlocks the door to McLuhan's imagination, flooding his parched mind with everything he knows he intuitively believes before he hears it from the mouths (and reads it in the works) of his greatest teachers. Their lectures – as well as their ground-breaking investigations and publications in the interconnected fields of the philosophies of rhetoric, literature, culture, and technology – profoundly shape McLuhan's lifelong scholastic attitudes, writerly approaches to style, and deeply held techno-cultural convictions.

Of these, none influences McLuhan more than *Practical Criticism*, a book in which Richards "exposes" the inadequacy of the Academy's outmoded approaches to "studying" literature in the twentieth century or *Culture and Environment*, perhaps the single most important Leavis volume McLuhan reads and certainly, as time reveals, the work most responsible for one of the young disciple's important breakthroughs. He discovers the ways in which the tools and analytic methods of the literary critic might bear fruit in other areas of investigation in the social sphere, in such unlikely stuff as advertisements, magazines, pamphlets, radio, newspapers, and the cinema.

The intermingling and wide-reaching approach Leavis recommends, a kind of cooperation between the worlds of science and literature, galvanizes McLuhan. Here, in all its glorious precision and exquisite simplicity, is the basis, the scaffolding, and the confirmation for the volume McLuhan dreams of writing, the one he'd imagined back on Gertrude Avenue, the Great Book that would reveal and illuminate the set of immutable laws of creation he's more and more convinced exist.

Thus, when Leavis suggests, in *Culture and Environment*, that the principles and practices of the New Criticism's emphasis on technical and formal investigation might similarly be employed when training in awareness of the social environment is required, McLuhan wholeheartedly embraces the notion, completely understanding its implications in terms of studying the forms, techniques, ways, means, and methods of the modern world (most easily observed in the new electric-electronic media increasingly making their presence felt in all areas of life).

Richards had similarly concerned himself with practicalities when he had conducted several literary experiments during his years as a professor. In the ones he describes at greatest length in *Practical Criticism*, he explains he presented numerous series of unsigned poems by unidentified authors to his students so they might critique them to assess their value and various merits. Richards had included both brilliant poems written by the art's greatest practitioners as well as banal poems penned by nobodies.

The students reviled the established writers' works and, far too frequently, waxed poetic on the virtues of the no-count entries. According to Richards, such gross misreadings demonstrated that an entirely new approach to literature was required. It was no longer enough, in the present world, to read, memorize, and regurgitate the received wisdom on the vague truth and beauty of what makes a poem (and poet) great. High-minded ideals and grand themes are well and good; but, the best way to approach a poem is through each of its words in relation to every other word it contains.

As far as Richards and ideas go, McLuhan intuitively grasps the notion that a good critic examines a poem in order to understand how (and why) it achieves its effects and successfully communicates with its readers through its words' various shades of meaning in terms of relationships, ambiguities, and resonances in the context of the poem itself.

Richards insists that literary criticism ought to focus on the meaning of words and the way in which they are used. He dismisses the "proper meaning superstition" as hogwash, primarily because words and their meanings are not independent of the way in which they are used. Words control thought. Their relationships create meaning since nothing has its meaning alone. A single note is not music. A single word is not a novel.

Additionally, McLuhan sees, a good critic examines what's on the page, not what's beyond it (in terms of who created it and why), in order to form sound judgments concerning its value. In other words, a good critic doesn't ask how a poem makes its readers feel; rather, a good critic explains why it makes them feel the way it does; or, more clearly, it's not what a poem "says" (its content or message) but how it's said or "presented" (its context or medium) in terms of the effect it has on a reader – also considered the cause of the poem since a poem only exists when it is being read – that really matters.

By the time McLuhan adds a second B.A. – this one from Cambridge – to his growing list of impressive credentials, he no longer feels he's beginning at the beginning. In fact, when he leaves the institution in 1936, his list of primary sources and influences has multiplied exponentially as he systematically ploughed through work after work with gusto and joy.

Not only does he find great solace and discover irrefutable support for his theories and beliefs in the French Symbolist poets and Cubist painters as well as the work of novelist James Joyce, economic-historian Harold Innis, poets T. S. Eliot and Ezra Pound, and painter-writer Wyndham Lewis, but he also begins his conversion to Roman Catholicism.

McLuhan prays for direction for two years before he converts. At one point, he writes to one of the Fathers at St. Louis University and asserts he does not "wish to take any step in it that is not consonant with the will of God... My increasing awareness has been of the ease with which Catholics can penetrate and dominate secular concerns – thanks to an emotional and spiritual economy denied to the confused secular mind." Later, he elaborates "there is no need to mention Christianity. It is enough that it be known that the operator is a Christian."

Yet, McLuhan's anxious, mostly because he worries about how his mother will deal with it. For her part, Elsie weeps copiously. Her eldest has ruined his chances to become a Great Man because Catholics are second-class nobodies in both business and education, at least as far as she's concerned. McLuhan dismisses her histrionic nay-saying; she, after all, has no inkling of the benefits and solace Catholicism bestows upon him, of the way it counteracts the effects of "that swift obliteration of the person which is going on."

For the first time in his spiritual life, he's at peace and deeply grateful for Catholicism. He believes an individual always maintains a constant nonstop dialogue with the Creator; and, "for that kind of dialogue, you don't need even to be verbal, let alone grammatical."

The kind of dialogue he would have with Marjorie's another matter entirely. Here, he most assuredly needs to be both verbal and demonstrative. As the months wear on, McLuhan's love for his perfect woman wears off, not surprisingly, considering time and distance factors.

At first, they write each other regularly, and he takes enormous pride in wearing the dashing scarves and colourful sweaters she knits for him; but, slowly, his feelings undergo a sea change. By the time he concludes his second year at Cambridge, McLuhan conceives of a way to break it to her gently, never dreaming his brilliant plan will backfire just as brilliantly.

He issues an ultimatum: Come to Cambridge now or forget it! Marjorie heads for England on the very next boat. Egads! This is not supposed to happen. The woman is supposed to refuse to visit, not to hop on the next thing sailing!

The pair spends some lovely times together, trekking around James Joyce's Dublin, biking through the English countryside, attending the cinema, dining by candlelight, and dancing to the beat of Joe Young's "Take My Heart," Irving Berlin's "Let Yourself Go," and Walter Hirsch's "Bye Bye Baby," but when Marjorie returns to Winnipeg, McLuhan admits to himself, somewhat guiltily, he's happy she's gone. A couple of months later, he writes the first love of his life a delicate Dear-Jane letter and reluctantly terminates the engagement.

If nothing else, McLuhan's time at Cambridge boosts his confidence and provides him with the kind of self-assurance he needs to pass the "tripos," the final English-literature examination that stands between him and his dreams. When he receives an upper second (second-class honours) instead of a first (straight As) on the exam, he feels diminished, unhappy, and deeply chagrined. More than anything else, he feels relief the ordeal's behind him (since exams have always been his Achilles heel).

Not without justification, McLuhan believes a graduate with a mere upper second cannot look forward to the benefits, advantages, and prestige a clean first provides; fortunately, his "poor" standing does not deter him in his quest to create a first-class body of work. After all, he reasons, if John Ruskin, who earned a fourth, had achieved greatness without the coveted first to aid him in his pursuits, the odds are in his favour that he, in possession of an upper second, will similarly accomplish great things.

By all accounts, McLuhan has come by his solid and sturdy strength of character honestly, several decades earlier, growing up deeply committed to excellence and wholly determined to make his mark. The young Canuck from the Prairies would, one way or another, indeed prove he was, in his mother's words, "clearly destined for greatness right around the globe."

3

A Professor is Born

> The role of advertising is not merely to sell good
> products but rather to confirm your own good
> judgement in buying them.
>
> — Marshall McLuhan

The live-it-up attitude of the 1920s' Jazz Age was, in
large part, responsible for the catastrophe looming
on the horizon of the next decade. With industry pro-
ducing vast quantities of assembly-line goods for the
first generation of women to embrace short skirts,
makeup, cigarettes, and alcohol as well as the first generation of mobile family men in need of the latest
inventions (radios, iceboxes, toasters, etc.) in automobiles to transport them to their offices, demand

McLuhan strikes a professorial pose
at Canada's Assumption College.

exceeds supply; but, short years later, the economy tanks, sinking demand.

Black Tuesday, the 29 October 1929 stock-market crash (complicated further by "dust-bowl" droughts in the West), first plunges the continent, then the globe, into the Great Depression.

This is a devastating time of mass hunger, homelessness, and poverty with unemployment rates skyrocketing from 9 to 30 per cent and wages plummeting by 60 per cent. When stock prices drop 40 per cent, hundreds of banks close their doors and wickets, thousands of businesses declare bankruptcy, and millions of dollars in savings accounts go up in smoke (or dust).

With goods aplenty but few buyers, one General Motors executive ruefully declares that economic prosperity cannot be maintained until producers, suppliers, and manufacturers cotton on to the notion that steady growth is only sustained by the organized creation of dissatisfaction among consumers through the development of seductive advertising and marketing techniques.

In rural Canada, low commodity prices and drought leave many farm families no option but to abandon their homes and seek salvation in the already overcrowded metropolitan centres where the destitute sleep in lean-to shanties wrapped in newspapers and, when the soup kitchens turn the starving away, scavenge for food in garbage bins.

When McLuhan regretfully says his final farewells to his friends and colleagues at his beloved Cambridge in 1936, he knows he's one of the lucky ones who's found employment. The job isn't much, not really, not in the grand scheme of what he'd hoped to be doing by the time he'd turned twenty-five. But, when Madison's University of Wisconsin offers him a teaching-assistant position in its English department paying seventy-five dollars a month, he jumps at the opportunity to live and work among students and faculty with a reputation for being lively, leftish, and intellectual. As long as they aren't Communists or homosexuals, he thinks, they and he will get along quite famously.

McLuhan, given the task of teaching twenty-five students a section of compulsory freshman English three times a week, balks. Grading papers? Parsing sentences? Discussing characters, settings, and themes of deadly dull novels, mostly written by Americans? TNT! (*Thanks, no thanks!*)

Rather than bore his students (and himself) with the same ol' same ol', McLuhan introduces them to the serious business of studying such items of popular culture as newspapers, comic books, advertisements, dimestore-detective novels, drugstore-romance magazines, and popular propaganda leaflets of the day.

At the same time, he sets up an "informal talk club" open to all teaching assistants. Both his students and colleagues, impressed by the erudite and articulate young professor-in-training who delivers lectures and speeches off the top of his head, admire his beautifully modulated tones and perfectly cultivated sentences and paragraphs, made all the more mesmerizing by the echoing lilt of a very faint British accent.

Once McLuhan settles into a routine of sorts at Wisconsin, his mental inventory of what he's accomplished impresses him not at all. He's bored (despite the

excitement his classes generate). He's also as tired of tus-
sling with colleagues and superiors as he's tired of wrangling with other graduate students over political power
points that have little to do with education and much too
much to do with getting ahead in the academic world.
He puts out feelers in an effort to find a more congenial
environment in which to teach, think, and write.

Ever industrious, given the mid-decade economic
realities and the lack of available positions, McLuhan
resolves to make the best of what turns out to be a dis-
appointing situation. He turns his hand to honing his
writing skills and penning articles for various academic
and literary journals. In these, he eloquently discourses
on subjects such as the importance of the thought of
recent Roman-Catholic convert G. K. Chesterton, the
respected English author of the sleuth/priest Father
Brown series of novels. McLuhan reveres him, as much
for his copacetic views on Catholicism as for his highly
playful and aphoristic style.

When McLuhan's Chesterton piece appears in a
quarterly published by Nova Scotia's Dalhousie
University, Father Gerald Phelan, the University of
Toronto's president of the Pontifical Institute of
Medieval Studies at St. Michael's College (and, incidentally, a friend of McLuhan's mother), impressed by
its contents, writes the first of several letters he sends
to the young Turk. It is the correspondence between
them – bolstered by a very satisfactory 1936 meeting
the pair enjoyed during McLuhan's Christmas holidays
spent in Toronto with Elsie and Red – that convinces
McLuhan he must do what he must do (despite the
unfavourable reaction he anticipates from his mother).

During his philosophical discussions (and spiritual
examinations) with Father Phelan, McLuhan more
than satisfies the priest his aim is true. Fifteen years
after his hero, G. K. Chesterton, converted to Roman
Catholicism, McLuhan is received into the Church on
30 March 1937.

After the deed is done, he writes and tells his parents of his decision, explaining how he's reached it.
Herb, in Winnipeg, takes his son's conversion in stride
and gives him his blessing. Elsie is beside herself, not
because the boy has abandoned her Church but
because, in her not-altogether-incorrect assessment of
the politics and prejudice of such things, Catholics
never receive the fancy prizes and promotions White
Anglo-Saxon Protestants (WASPs) consider their
birthright. Elsie's dreams for her son bite the dust as
she struggles to come to grips with the fact that by
becoming a Catholic he's ensured he'll never be
appointed the president of the University of Toronto,
let alone Harvard.

To his credit, McLuhan assures his mother he's
well aware of the political implications of his decision.
He points out he's already made a pact with himself
that ensures he'll never stoop to either discussing or
promoting his faith in public. He is not, he insists, a
theologian on a mission to bring converts into the
Church. For him, religion is a personal decision, a private affair, not a public spectacle.

Simply, McLuhan loves the rituals, the majesty,
the processions, the dignity, and the celebration of the
seven sacraments, particularly the Eucharist, the
prayerful sublimity of the consecrated Body and Blood

of Christ. He considers the act of partaking of the Host as necessary to him as the air he breathes. He additionally views The Sacrifice of the Mass as the greatest form of theatre possible, as the only form of theatre in which the audience participates (or, more specifically, in which the audience no longer exists as audience).

Pious but not pompous, McLuhan believes that hell exists, a fire-and-brimstone place he has no plans to visit; at least, not if he can help it. He occasionally wonders why priests don't mention hell more frequently, why they don't understand the value of putting the fear of hell into their parishioners, recognizing that just as newspapers and magazines sell bad ("real") news in order to sell good news (advertisements), Catholicism might likewise benefit from selling bad news (hell) in order to celebrate good news (the gospel).

Dejected over his lack of prospects in Wisconsin, McLuhan takes comfort in meditation and finds strength in prayer. Mostly, he prays to the Virgin (with whom he feels a special affinity). In particularly trying times, he addresses his petitions to Saint Jude, the patron saint of lost and hopeless causes.

In this instance, McLuhan's prayers are answered.

Good news comes his way.

He's just heard from Missouri's St. Louis University – a Jesuit institution and the best Catholic university in the United States – that he's landed the job of instructor in its Department of English headed up by a Cambridge man, Dr. William McCabe, S. J. Not even the discovery of the university's inferior library nor his paltry salary, only slightly better than what he earns at Wisconsin, dampens McLuhan's spirits, most likely because the great – if not eccentric – Dr. Bernard J. Muller-Thym, one of the truly original Medieval scholars of the time, also on faculty at St. Louis, befriends him.

Legend has it Muller-Thym, the epitome of absent-mindedness, forgets to pull on a pair of pants before leaving his apartment one fine morning; legend further has it, when guests are invited for dinner and Muller-Thym's wife features spaghetti on the menu, he passes around damp bath towels instead of more conventional serviettes or napkins.

None of this fazes McLuhan in the slightest. He and Muller-Thym spend a great deal of time together, arguing about most everything, agreeing only on one point: Their solid friendship means a great deal to both men.

It's Muller-Thym, in fact, who introduces McLuhan to the rich and variegated life and culture of the Middle Ages. Muller-Thym also conveys his theory concerning the way in which the human senses work to McLuhan. Such ideas and theories, which McLuhan had previously gleaned from reading the poetry of Gerard Manley Hopkins and T. S. Eliot, for example, confirm for him his own understanding of the way in which an individual experiences the world through an intertwingling of all senses working in cooperative harmony to provide any given experience with logic and coherence.

McLuhan gets to work, teaching not only freshman English but also courses in Milton, Shakespeare, and the English Renaissance as well as introducing his students to the principles of the New Criticism he'd learned during his Cambridge years. Too, he returns to the task of writing articles, this time penning, for instance, "Peter or Peter Pan?" for the university's literary journal, *Fleur de Lis*. It's a spirited invective in which he denounces advertising, industrialism, big business, and Marxism while pitting Saint Peter (the good news) against immature Peter-Pan fantasies fostered by far too many sissified and mollycoddled contemporaries (the bad news). It sets the tone for McLuhan's discourse over the next decade or so.

Ever-ready in the party department, McLuhan develops close friendships with several other members of the university community but comes to feel particularly comfortable playing charades, aiming darts, tossing beanbags, or engaging in heated debates with fast friends Karl and Addie Strohbach.

"Right," adds Addie. "If you had a sarcastic sense of humour you could twist something he said around, and he loved that. Then, he would twist what *you* said around and show where you were wrong. He liked that kind of thing because it gave him a second platform for his argument."

The delightfully gifted and gracefully gorgeous Corinne Keller Lewis, a twenty-six-year-old drama and speech teacher as well as a student actress, travels from Fort Worth, Texas to California's Pasadena Playhouse to further her education during the summer of 1938. There, she meets fellow-thespian Elsie McLuhan, herself studying acting. Elsie, it seems, is the mother of one very eligible and highly motivated bachelor who, it turns out, is planning a trek to Los Angeles's Huntington Library to further his research on Elizabethan satirist and journalist Thomas Nashe, the subject of his Ph.D. dissertation.

∞

"Miss Corinne Lewis, it gives me great pleasure to formally introduce you to my eldest son, soon-to-be Dr. Herbert Marshall McLuhan, the esteemed…"

"… Marshall, Mother, Marshall. *Please*. How do you do, Miss Lewis? I'm as pleased as punch to make your acquaintance; Mother has told me such wonderful things about you!"

"All true, too, Marshall. Corinne graduated from Texas Christian University and has been teaching in ʾort Worth since 1935. Her family lives there, you know? A traditional Southern family, no less."

"You don't say? How, Miss Lewis, would your traditional Southern family feel about nomadic Northerners such as Mother and yours truly?"

"Well… Of course, my family would feel… Why do you ask?"

"I ask because, believe it or not, I was wondering if your traditional Southern family would object terribly if I escorted you to Catalina Island where you and I might enjoy the sites and scenery of that fabled locale."

"And?"

"Well, if your family didn't consider the prospect too odious, I thought we could make a weekend of it since, as you no doubt know, all work and no play means Miss Lewis will have no fun unless I rescue her from the clutches of my meddling marriage-minded mother."

"Well, we wouldn't want that, now, would we, Mr. McLuhan?"

"Dear Miss Lewis, please. I would be honoured if you would join me; and, I would be most thrilled if you simply called me Marshall."

"Marshall, right now, I cannot possibly even think of anything I'd rather do than accompany you to Catalina."

"Mother?"

"Wonderful! Excellent! While you and Corinne relax on Catalina, I fully intend to spend the weekend working on my tan and savouring several less-than-edifying gossip sheets, if that doesn't offend the sensibilities of the young lovers, of course."

"Elsie!"

"Mother!"

"Marshall! Corinne!... *Bon voyage*, Darlings."

∞

On 4 August 1939, after a frenzied search for both suitable rings and a marriage licence, Corinne and Marshall McLuhan wed in St. Louis's Catholic cathedral before making their way to New York to board the ocean liner that takes the honeymooners to Italy and France.

Their memories of that idyllic time – visiting the graves of Keats and Shelley, drifting along in a gondola drinking in the sights of Venice by moonlight, and strolling through historic Paris parks and museums – increasingly shore them up against a world that will soon come tumbling down around them. The blisstatic McLuhans settle in a Cambridge ravaged by the Great Depression just as the Second World War breaks out.

Establishing themselves for the next two years, the newlyweds find agreeable accommodations near the university, and Cambridge's newest research student begins work on his dissertation, spending much of his time in the Rare Books Room of the university's library, reading widely and deeply. The couple copies out long passages from the hundreds of works that bear directly upon McLuhan's research and investigations into the life, times, contemporaries, and writings of Thomas Nashe, the subject of his thesis.

McLuhan regularly bikes through England's southern counties, memorizing important information and key passages from Nashe's various works. After spending their days in the library, the McLuhans work together on the evening meals and dishes before reading aloud to each other or perfecting their dart-board skills. In 1940, acutely mindful of rations, shortages, and the war effort, his wife knits. He unwinds by the fire, puffing contentedly on his pipe (filled with the only luxury he allows himself, his favourite choice brand of tobacco), contemplating his latest research discoveries, finding himself becoming increasingly intoxicated with Nashe's droll, colloquial, and sensuous style.

Heavily marked by puns and pyrotechnic word-play, Nashe's way with words suitably impresses the language-loving McLuhan. When he discovers no less than the great Irish novelist James Joyce himself (*A Portrait of the Artist as a Young Man, Ulysses, Finnegans Wake*) had taken the polemical journalist as his model, McLuhan's admiration for Nashe's rambunctious style goes through the roof.

Still, as his readings proceed, he finds himself running smack-dab into the same brick walls of knowledge again and again; the more he reads, the clearer it becomes that Nashe's work owes much of its vigour and brilliance to the theories and practices of the ancients (e.g., Cicero, Seneca, and Quintilian as well as the various Stoics). And, once he reads Morris W. Croll's Preface to John Lyly's *Euphues*, he decides nothing less than a full-scale examination of primary sources is required.

Perusing translations of passages of analogues created three centuries before the birth of Christ and based upon the satirical work of Menippus (who himself drew inspiration from Diogenes' cynic philosophy), McLuhan observes each fragment's argument is indeed carefully structured along classical lines in the spirit of the great Roman models. He additionally notes every fragment's written in a sarcaustic style that mocks ideas, institutions, and conventions in a dialogue alternating between prose and verse passages.

Digging deeper, he unearths the roots of the ancients' trivium (logic, rhetoric, and grammar). Their tree of knowledge is comprised of these three branches with each representing a unique worldview with its own set of assumptions built into it. The branch of logic depends on critical reasoning; that of rhetoric

involves the fivefold art of persuasion (inventio, dispo-
sitio, pronuntiatio, elocutio, and memoria); and, grammar's branch highlights the belief that language creates
thought and, by extension, meaning and coherence.
The Stoics, who conceived of the science of grammar –
the study of words and their arrangements – began
with the premise that the universe itself, also known as
Logos, is the divine word.

Once language's secrets are fully revealed,
McLuhan reasons, the heart of its universe will wholly
open. To put it plainly, he begins to understand that
the code of Western culture – or what he still loosely
considers the universe's immutable laws he'd first
glimpsed back on Gertrude Avenue – can only be
cracked by firmly grasping the shifting nature of the
relationships among logic, rhetoric, and grammar.

Ha! Easier said than done!

McLuhan, allowing himself a rare moment of self-
satisfaction in spite of himself, smiles expansively,
breathes deeply, and confidently rolls up his sleeves in
preparation for what will surely become the task of his
intellectual life.

Upon their return to St. Louis in 1940, the McLuhans
rent a bright and spacious three-bedroom apartment
on Maryland Street. It's a good name for a street, at
least as far as McLuhan's concerned. Any street that
causes a person to think of the blessed Virgin's bound
to be a very good street, particularly if the person in
question has just returned from passing around cele-

bratory cigars to his friends and colleagues at the university, especially since the person has just become the first-time father of one highly vocal little guy, Thomas Eric Marshall McLuhan, born 19 January 1942.

It is there, on Maryland Street, with no end to the war in sight, that McLuhan experiences the first of a number of what James Joyce termed epiphanies (defining and clarifying moments when the heart of the truth of an object, an individual, or a situation is revealed).

It changes the course of his life.

Wyndham Lewis's highly unusual but indubitably
original sketch created during McLuhan's
Assumption College sojourn.

4

Going Places

Competition creates resemblance... Profes-
sionalism is following the leader.
— Marshall McLuhan

McLuhan's first epiphany occurs when he realizes
his days at St. Louis University are numbered. He
will have to act decisively. He will have to complete his
dissertation as quickly as possible.

Oh, he finds some small satisfactions teaching
– and supervising the theses of – the brighter students
on campus. The engaging and brilliant minds of several
faculty members with whom he becomes friends also
provide him with satisfying intellectual company as
well as extremely valuable insights into his own

scholarly pursuits that later prove indispensable in his own work.

The reasons for this epiphany? The low pay, the lack of prestige, the heavy teaching load, and the unsympathetic chairman of the department who's replaced his friend and ally, William McCabe, not to mention his growing family and increasingly well-founded worries concerning the draft.

In December 1943, the Canadian is indeed classified "1-A" despite wife and child. McLuhan's relieved to concurrently learn he's received his Cambridge Ph.D., which assures him of immediate promotion from instructor to assistant professor, a title that enhances his appeal to prospective employers in his chosen field.

At an impromptu gathering held in honour of his achievement, McLuhan thanks his best graduate students, Maurice McNamee (for teaching him a great deal about Frances Bacon and his love of the pithy aphorism) as well as Walter Ong (for writing his thesis, *Ramus, Method, and the Decay of Dialogue*, from which McLuhan learns a great deal concerning the cultural, social, and perceptual changes resulting from the invention of the printing press in Strasbourg in the 1430s by a goldsmith named Johannes Gutenberg).

He also attempts to placate those colleagues he alienated at St. Louis, the ones who find his one-sidedness bothersome, boorish, and dismissive, the ones who claim all McLuhan really needs is a stooge or silent partner present in the room while he thinks aloud:

"I have to engage in endless dialogue before I write," McLuhan explains, "I want to *talk* a subject over and over... I do a lot of my serious work while I'm talking out loud to people. I'm feeling around, not making pronouncements. Most people use speech as a result of thought, but I use it as the process."

His first batch of detractors puts on deaf airs when it comes to the subject of Dr. Herbert Marshall McLuhan, the university's rising star whose startling and stimulatingly refreshing articles are snagging stellar marks and flattering remarks. The erudite and articulate editors and readers of both the *Sewanee* and *Kenyon Reviews*, champions of the Southern school of New Criticism (including John Crowe Ransom, Allen Tate, Cleanth Brooks, Robert Penn Warren, et al.), love the guy.

McLuhan handily catches the attention of the audience he hopes to attract by publishing "Dagwood's America" in *Columbia* (1944), a controversial article in which he cites Blondie as the symbolic head of the American family responsible for turning Dagwood into little more than an emasculated footnote: "Blondie and her children own America, control American business and entertainment, run hog-wild in spreading maternalism into education and politics."

To ensure a man remains manly, that man must secure "healthy and fructifying work" and avoid the fate of finding himself reduced to one of sixty million Dagwoodian mama's boys. To accomplish this, advises McLuhan, a wholesale reclamation of "the detached use of autonomous reason for the critical appraisal of life" is in order.

In an effort to build upon his early publication successes and to obtain maximum exposure, McLuhan next submits an article of social criticism – "Is Post-War Polygamy Inevitable?" – to the editors at *Esquire*. In it, he warns such phenomena as rising divorce rates, sexual promiscuity, the adoption of illegitimate children, and artificial insemination are destabilizing forces corrupting and eroding the values of the nuclear family. Industry, consumerism, and the increasing necessity for double-income families will turn both men and women into little more than robotic wage-slaves who are, in essence, free to do what they are told.

The editors *pooh-pooh* his dire ruminations and reject his article posthaste.

By contrast, *The Sewanee Review*'s editors welcome McLuhan's lively, original, and colourful contributions, particularly relishing "Footprints in the Sands of Crime," wherein the sleuth's sleuth connects the sleuthery of Sherlock Holmes and Edgar Allan Poe with the works of Cicero and the Renaissance humanists via the work of the romantic (Byron) and symbolist (Baudelaire) poets.

It is, in fact, in this same article that McLuhan elaborates on the theme of another of his epiphanies, this one involving Poe's story (and the course of his own life), "A Descent into the Maelstrom." He explains the sailor caught in the whirlpool saves himself from drowning by calmly examining the vortex and coolly observing its effects. In the story, Poe's survivor reveals he "became obsessed with the keenest curiosity about the whirl itself. I positively felt a wish to explore its depths, even at the sacrifice I was going to make; and, my principal grief was that I should never be able to tell my old companions on shore about the mysteries I should see."

McLuhan sees his own work exactly as the sailor sees the vortex or as the sleuthing detective who seeks for clues and motives sees the scene of the crime. His job is to unearth causes, observe effects, and accurately report upon them. "Poe's sailor saved himself by studying the action of the whirlpool and by cooperating with it."

∽

It will be the last year the family spends in St. Louis. Having made the transition from literary to social and cultural critic, McLuhan's amplified restlessness and nervousness vis-à-vis exiting the country are calmed, somewhat, by the appearance of English painter, novelist, and critic, Wyndham Lewis, on the horizon.

McLuhan's mother, now residing in Detroit, Michigan and working as a director with that city's Drama Study Club, alerts her son to the legendary individual's present term of employment at Windsor's Assumption College. Thanks mostly to the compassion and largesse of Father J. Stanley Murphy who, after Lewis introduces him to the up-and-coming scholar, offers the young star the position of head of the English department at Assumption College, McLuhan sees his way cleared to return to Canada and move on to the next level. Father Stan assures McLuhan the time shall be found for him to continue work on his first book (which he'd finally started writing in St. Louis).

It takes about a second to make up his mind. The McLuhan family makes a beeline for the Canadian border, boisterous Eric happily chatting in tow.

Unhappily, McLuhan's Windsor sojourn is not all he hopes it will be. Certainly, he gains some solace and satisfaction from his association with one of the kindest and most generous human beings McLuhan will meet, Father Stan. He also discovers he and Lewis – despite the impossibly difficult personage's high-strung personality and his vicious predilection for insulting McLuhan as someone "sick with unsatisfied vanity" – share a number of agreeable affinities, particularly when their discussions converge in terms of the way both thinkers view the world around them.

"Lewis, Old Sport, you just might be right. You just might be right about that hallucinatory trance, that waking sleep."

"Indubitably... The world is in the strictest sense asleep, with rare intervals and spots of awareness. It is almost the sleep of the insect or the animal world."

"Oh, yeah! You can say that again. But, it's those intervals, those 'rare intervals,' that make it all worthwhile, isn't it? You know, I'm sorry you're leaving, Lewis, I'm a gonna miss you when you and the missus leave us back here with the hicks in the sticks in the wilds of Windsor. I might even find it in my heart to forgive you for leaving my right eye and the top of my head out of that gawddawful charcoal sketch of yours... I might even find it in my heart to forgive you sometime soon, especially since I'm considering having the blasted thing framed. Now, don't you go thinking I *have* forgiven you, not quite yet! Only time will tell. Speaking of, what time's your departure?"

"Tomorrow morning, crack of dawn. And, I don't give two hoots whether you forgive me or not, Mac Ol'

Boy. Forgiveness is for sinners. I am a saint, albeit a self-condemned one... Actually, I'm lying. Father Murphy's the saint. The next time I'm in Rome, I shall undoubtedly make the Pope aware of that very important saintly fact."

"Oh, you've got an audience with His Holiness?"

"Heavens, no! No, no, no, Marshall. His Holiness has an audience with me!"

"Balls!"

Approximately 150 students register at Assumption College in the autumn of 1944. That December, Father Murphy's cautiously hopeful. He surveys his office, slowly twirling around the small room in his rich and splendid leather chair, his faculty's Christmas gift to him. *Well, there's the Christian Culture series presenting artists and writers of international fame and acclaim. It's garnering lots of attention in the media. There's noted philosopher Jacques Maritain. He's generously agreed to waive his fees to show his support for our cash-strapped college. Thankfully, Mr. and Mrs. Lewis have had a safe trip home; and, at present, the family of the new head of the Department of English is settling quite nicely in a stately old farmhouse out on the Tecumseh Road beyond the city limits...*

"Father?... Father Stan?"

"Marshall?!"

"Nothing like scaring a daydreaming cleric lost in thought, eh? Guess what? Now that we're going to be parents again – get this – Corinne's teaching me to drive

– er, make that, Corinne's *trying* to teach me to drive –
out on the farm. I had my first lesson last night, in fact."

"And?"

"And, I thoroughly blew it! Big bust! I kept jam-
ming on the brakes and flooring the accelerator. So,
Corinne says, 'Well, Marsh, since you can't get out of
second gear, perhaps we should try teaching you how
to go into reverse.' I couldn't get out of second gear,
right? Then, she's teaching me to go in reverse, right?"

"Right. And?"

"And… Well, I backed into our cow, our lovely
Jersey cow."

"Oh, dear…"

"Oh, the cow's fine, Father. I'm a wreck; but, the
cow's just fine. In fact, when I got up this morning? I
swear, the cow's milk was even sweeter than ever!"

"What does Corinne think?"

"Corinne? Oh, she's not so sure; she thinks the
cow's milk always tastes sweet. And, she also thinks
buses are a truly marvellous modern invention. Funnily
enough, I totally agree with her."

"Funnily enough, Marsh, so do I."

When McLuhan is not "devising barricades against the
insolent ingenuity of Eric," working on the manuscript
for his first book, writing to Wyndham Lewis about
"the terrible social cowardice" comprising "the mental
vacuum that is Canada," dealing with the added and
seemingly endless responsibilities of running the
department as well as teaching rhetoric and the princi-

ples of the New Criticism, frantically gathering notes for papers and talks he must deliver and articles he must write (and which his wife must type for him), the man of boundless energy spends his free time walking the lanes and exploring the countryside along the Tecumseh Road.

"What a bee-yoo-tee-full sight!"

A full-blown rip-snortin' tornado, whipping across the bottom of the farmers' fields about two hundred metres south, creeps closer and closer to the McLuhan home. McLuhan and a buddy are snapping pictures with a camera, standing in front of the house where the rest of the family's huddled in the basement. Then, suddenly, the tornado seems to freeze just before it veers west, whisking along the Tecumseh Road, impervious to the farmer racing alongside it and firing shots into its funnel. It swallows up houses and barns and snaps the Tecumseh River bridge from its moorings. Then, just as quickly as it appears, it disintegrates as it reaches the river's edge.

"We saw it collapse ever so leisurely, beautifully. Like the Indian rope-trick. Something out of *The Arabian Nights*. Bee-yoo-tee-full!"

On 26 October 1945, mere weeks before the conclusion of World War II, the twins, Teresa Carolyn and Mary Corinne, arrive within seven minutes of each other, much to the delight of highly precocious big-brother Eric. His mother, naturally, is both filled with relief and flooded with joy. His father, although thrilled

with the appearance of his lovely daughters, is preoccupied, obsessed almost, with finding ways to provide for his growing family, something he determines will be next-to-impossible to accomplish if he remains in Windsor earning, on average, approximately twenty-five hundred dollars per year.

No Dagwood he, McLuhan takes his role as breadwinner seriously, but either because he's preoccupied with his career or because he cringes recalling elements of his own harrowing childhood, McLuhan proves to be something of a dud in the Dad department.

He whines about how long it takes to feed a pair of babies. He gripes about Eric's exploratory rambunctiousness (despite the fact he's gone so far as to bolt a window-screen across the top of the little escape artist's playpen). When he takes his turns doing the laundry, McLuhan invariably grumbles something vaguely rude about how much he hates washing-machines, about how they're such an invasion in the home, about the way they make people mechanical slaves, nothing more than sanitation-detail servomechanisms, yadda yadda yadda.

Behind every great man, there's an even greater woman. McLuhan's wife is no exception. Pauline Bondy, a friend of the family in Windsor, remembers McLuhan "would invite anybody to stay with them. He would invite the dean of Ely Cathedral, who happened to be in town, to stay with them, when they had no spare room at all for him. They would put the dean of Ely on the chesterfield to sleep. As long as there was a hunk of bread in the kitchen he would invite people to stay. Sometimes it was hard on Corinne's pride."

To her credit, the indomitable young mother gracefully takes it all in stride. She understands when her husband hits the lecture circuit before travelling to Toronto in the spring of 1946 to be formally offered the teaching position in the Department of English at Canada's premier university. She understands why, two years after the family's move to Tecumseh Road, the post is so important to his work, his career, and his prestige, not to mention his monthly take-home pay.

That day, she also ensures his meagre travelling kit, consisting primarily of a toothbrush and a shaving kit, is complemented by at least one change of socks and underwear. She's well aware McLuhan will think nothing of not wearing socks at all if clean socks are not to be had, given his tendency to willfully degenerate into whole-hog slobbery at the drop of a hat. She believes he's almost cured of his habit of eating left-overs from the plates of others. And, as for that old piece of cheese he often carries around in his brief-case? Well, she can almost accept her congenitally undomesticated husband's explanation it just improves with age. Almost.

Corinne Lewis McLuhan, well aware, in her own way, of the fact her husband, in his own way, deeply appreciates her talents, efforts, and unqualified support, often overhears her man bragging about her compassion, understanding, patience, loyalty, beauty, even-handedness, terrific dictation and typing skills, house-hold-managerial abilities bar none, and marvellous sense of humour. Once, while selling off a double bed the couple has shared, the truly great dame makes an unforgettable impression upon one of the university's seminarians when she remarks it's a fact of life the springs don't last long on any bed she and McLuhan share.

∽

While in Toronto regarding the paltry perks and more agreeable financial terms of his prestigious appointment, the university's freshest face readily accepts the offer to rent a three-bedroom flat with a pair of fireplaces at 91 St. Joseph Street, a brisk hop, step, and jingle from St. Michael's College with several beautiful parks he loves visiting in close proximity. During this brief reconnaissance mission, McLuhan arranges for Latin and Greek lessons for four-year-old Eric (since, as McLuhan himself acknowledges, Eric is now more fully self-possessed and less given to bouts of "snide propositions and concupiscent sophistries"). McLuhan also puts his highly developed investigative skills to good use learning the behind-the-scenes ins-and-outs of the department he will join later that year.

During one of his lectures just before he takes up his St. Michael's position, McLuhan is introduced to a distinguished professor of English from the University of Toronto's Victoria College, the soon-to-be-celebrated author of *Fearful Symmetry: A Study of William Blake*, Dr. Northrop Frye. McLuhan notes with satisfaction his own soon-to-published work – variously titled "Guide to Chaos," "Typhon in America," "Folklore of Industrial Man," "Jitterbugs of the Absolute," "Sixty Million Mama's Boys," and "The Mechanical Bride," – also bears scrutiny in relation to Blake's writings.

He is favourably impressed with the achievements of many of the members of the department he will soon join, and his sleuthing also proves valuable, if only because it encourages the black-and-white thinker to temper his tendency to view the world with little regard for subtle shades of grey:

"I know what to expect," he thoughtfully reflects. "*But*, some very good students are there. That's all one can ask. A few good colleagues, good library, good music, and good students. Also a living wage, fine surrounds and suitable circumstances for raising children."

If McLuhan knows what to expect, his current employer, Father Murphy, likewise nurtures his own set of expectations concerning the loss of his highly entertaining friend as well as the departure of one of Assumption College's brightest faculty members in recent history.

After all, it's not every day a scholar of McLuhan's stature comes along, and to his everlasting credit, Father Murphy readily acknowledges it was crystal clear to him from the get-go the silver-tongued sage of the electronic age was destined for unprecedented success on a far grander scale on a far greater international stage where, predicts Father Stan, McLuhan's ultimately headed (whether he's fully aware of that fact himself quite yet or not).

Back in Toronto, Marshall and Corinne McLuhan show off their four daughters (Mary, Teresa, Elizabeth, and Stephanie).

5

The Doctor is In

Anyone who takes time to study the techniques of pictorial reportage in the popular press and magazines will easily find a dominant pattern composed of sex and technology. Hovering around this pair will usually be found images of hectic speed, mayhem, violence, and sudden death.

– Marshall McLuhan

St. Michael's College, still hovering between two worlds in 1946, is loyally committed to its Catholic Basilian tradition but not entirely indifferent to its reputation as an institution of second-rate scholastic importance. In bringing McLuhan – and another layman of equal brilliance, philosopher Lawrence Lynch –

into the fold, the college's Powers-That-Be take posi-
tive steps towards improving St. Mike's standing and
esteem among the federations within the university
community.

Other colleges – the Anglican Trinity, the United-
Methodist Victoria (home to critic and scholar
Northrop Frye), and the secular University College –
pay their faculty members approximately a thousand
more dollars a month than the annual forty-five hundred dollars McLuhan earns at St. Mike's, for example.
(At this time, a new car sells for fourteen hundred dollars while gasoline costs sixteen cents a gallon; and, the
McLuhans already pay the college sixty-five dollars per
month in rent for their St. Joseph Street home.)

Still, McLuhan's salary makes it possible for him
to acquire a half-share in a beat-up sailboat for himself
and growing family; plus, mostly for his wife's use, he
negotiates a good deal on an old Plymouth, an automobile that had rolled off the assembly line in 1929.
Throughout his life, McLuhan's wife manages his funds
and provides him with an allowance. As a result, he's
mindful of his nickels and dimes and constantly on the
lookout for a good bargain. Not surprisingly, he finds it
almost impossible to back down during a price-setting
haggle session.

As far as modern labour-saving devices go? These
impress him not at all, a fact which so exasperates his
wife she's reduced to borrowing a neighbour's vacuum
cleaner, a fact which so exasperates her husband he's
forced to soothe his wounded pride by applying his
well-developed bargaining skills – learned from his
mother during the Great Depression – to haggle pas-

sionately with the Hoover salesman over the price he'll pay for one of the dreadful noise-making contraptions also known as mechanical slave-makers, mere servo-mechanizers...

Natch, when television comes to Canada in the early 1950s, the McLuhans are the last on the block to own a set (which is promptly placed in the basement so the monster doesn't dominate the living room, already positively dominated by the comforting glow of embers in the fireplace). McLuhan, never a big television watcher at the best of times, nonetheless keeps up with its programming and development. He also tells his friends and colleagues he believes impressionable young minds shouldn't be subjected to television's druglike properties for more than one hour per week.

In the epiphany department, McLuhan's latest, as mundane as it is pressing, concerns his finances and future prospects, namely, acquiring a full professorship as well as tenure. One of his associates, not altogether impressed with the Cambridge man's self-confident attitude, highly unusual teaching methods, and intellectual brilliance – perhaps because McLuhan routinely refers to the associate's circle of colleagues as a "ghastly crew" – chattily recounts the details of the substance of a conversation the pair's just concluded:

"He said to me, 'You know, going to Assumptio. locked me into the Roman Catholic network because nobody in the outside world would ever look to Assumption for a scholar.' That was true. There was a prejudice pretty well in every university in Canada against employing Roman Catholics – and especially Catholics who had announced their Catholicism by being employed in a Catholic institution. So McLuhan felt trapped. He had come from Assumption to the top Catholic college in Canada – and where could he go from there?"

Where, indeed?

∞

In June 1948, McLuhan would go to New York to visit the cosmopolitan city already considered the centre of artistic, intellectual, and commercial activity right around the globe. Occasionally despairing over the boondocks mentality of both Toronto's citizenry and its famed university's thinkers who view culture as "basically, an unpleasant moral duty," he experiences half an urge to live and work permanently in New York in order to circulate among its influential magazine editors and book publishers, not to mention its advertising offices lining Madison Avenue.

After he settles into a nondescript New York hotel room, McLuhan inks the first of many publishing contracts and accepts an advance of $250 for his debut work, a book he's recently taken to calling "The Folklore of Industrial Man."

∞

Mcluhan's publisher, prestigious Vanguard Press, expects the newbie author will continue his work on the effects of advertisements and advertising by writing an explosive exposé to end all exposés on the subject. The publisher assumes McLuhan will tear the hide off the ad-men for manipulating and hoodwinking consumers into believing the most outlandish claims about the various products and services their advertising gambits shamelessly promote. And, the publisher quite reasonably expects McLuhan's manuscript will contain several hundred double-spaced neatly typed pages presenting a cogent point-by-point argument which brings to light the effects advertising achieves as it goes about its business of creating what the General Motors executive calls organized dissatisfaction.

When the cardboard box McLuhan submits is unwrapped, the publisher's deeply dismayed to discover five-hundred manuscript pages paper-clipped together with hundreds of aging newspaper and magazine ads and articles. The editor assigned to work with McLuhan on his manuscript is in shock:

"I was even afraid to show the manuscript to anybody, because it seemed to me that it was going to require so much work... But there was something intriguing about it. No matter where you picked it up, one of the paragraphs was fascinating. And we finally decided that it was just a question of finding some way to do it, of just making a good selection. [The publisher] always thought of the book as a kind of exposé of advertising because he did enjoy exposé books and had a history of publishing them. I knew it certainly wasn't that, but I went along with the treatment of it as that because it was getting at something which I thought was tremendously valuable."

The editor soon discovers the manuscript contains a critique of the whole of Western culture. It reveals the grand design supporting everything from the illusions of perfumes, pet-food, and Plymouth advertisements to the fantasies underlying shoot-'em-up movies, super-hero comics, and glossy fashion magazines. In her opinion, there's definitely an important book among the clippings and massively sprawling manuscript in that cardboard box; the question is, Where exactly is this book?

McLuhan sees the book, that's a fact, even if his editor and publisher do not. It takes a great deal of time and an immense editorial effort to find the book McLuhan insists is right there. The process drives McLuhan around the bend as he enters into endless back-and-forth skirmishes and counter-skirmishes that include pleading, wheedling, scheming, and screaming tactics. Some of the tactics backfire. Others work wonders. All create a protracted struggle over the manuscript. The tug-of-wills takes its toll. McLuhan develops chronic and searing headaches as a result of the tensions.

In 1950, while the manuscript for *The Mechanical Bride: The Folklore of Industrial Man* is prepped for publication, the McLuhans are again on the move, this time taking up residence in what had once been the college infirmary at 81 St. Mary's Street, as run-down, lived-in, and comfortably dilapidated as any of the previous homes the family's occupied in St. Louis or Windsor. With the arrival of Stephanie Lewis (14 October 1947) and Elizabeth Anne (2 August 1950), the time for a house, even a house with a front door that never quite shuts properly, is right.

The logistics of the move are expertly handled by the budding author's wife. Corinne McLuhan attends to the various details involved in efficiently relocating the worldly goods of the family's seven members. Meanwhile, the budding author, preoccupied with the preparation of the manuscript, spends much of his time attempting to satisfy editorial demands for cuts, changes, and rewrites on the work which, Vanguard assures its very frustrated budding author, will most certainly be published in the fall of 1951, just in time for the Christmas rush.

Despite its provocative title (inspired by Marcel Duchamp's mysterious 1915-1923 masterpiece, *The Bride Stripped Bare by Her Bachelors, Even*), the first printing of *The Mechanical Bride* sells no more than a few hundred copies, even though it receives a handful of fairly respectable and generally favourable reviews in the media. A couple of pundits refer to McLuhan's "tonnes of rich and purple baloney" or take great pains to point out the rookie writer has borrowed "the same razzle-dazzle technique in his presentation that the admen themselves have mastered with such advantage." More charitable commentators applaud "the significant social document" for its "full-blooded thumps."

Chastened by its failure, McLuhan buys up one thousand copies of the book after its price is drastically reduced due to its poor performance. Surrounded by these copies, he thinks long and hard about what's gone wrong and finally concludes he will never write another book like it, deciding it's little more than pop-cult science fiction with comic strips and ads cast as characters; in other words, he'll no longer rant and rave about the negative effects of capitalism, commercialism, consumerism, industrialism, dialectical materialism, mechanistic automatism, or any of the other *Isms* he's devoted this past decade to attacking.

In another epiphanous moment, McLuhan understands *The Mechanical Bride*'s biggest problem: He has, he notes, come down too heartily on the side of the individual and raged too heavily against the age of machines. Disappointed but undaunted, he swears he will never again make the error of critical moralism and will, in future efforts, adopt the stance of the detached observer.

From this moment on, he will comment as clearly and accurately as he can on the world as he finds it. Further, civilized detachment, not moral regret, is the only plausible reaction to the fragmentation of the electric age. The industrial era draws to a close while the age of what he will soon call "the new tribalism" emerges.

It is not for him, he deduces, to pronounce on what is wrong. His role, the one he understands he must adopt for the rest of his writerly life, is to report on what he sees happening in the world as accurately and objectively as possible. Is he not the new and improved version of Poe's sailor who coolly examines the whirlpool's action in order to escape its deadly effects? And, if anyone asks why he calls his book *The Mechanical Bride*?

He'll tell the truth, short, sweet, and to the point:

The book's about the death of sex.

That's right, S-E-X.

As the pioneering psychiatrist Sigmund Freud observed, 92 per cent of everything's about sex.

Advertising turns consumers into eternally frustrated voyeurs of the visible yet chronically unattainable (or, to put it more succinctly still, advertising has succeeded in putting pleasure to work for it in its quest to create a highly lucrative state of organized dissatisfaction in the all-important marketplace).

Sex was killed (or, more accurately, rendered an artificially scarce commodity) by advertising when Madison Avenue started using its universal appeal to sell any and every little thing. Through mass media, even the most sexless of objects or products have become sexualized (from vehicles, cleaning products, and popular music to cigarettes, disposable diapers, and household appliances).

That year, in one of his many letters to American writer Ezra Pound (whom he'd visited during the poet's incarceration for treason at St. Elizabeth's Hospital for the Criminally Insane in Washington, DC), McLuhan again refers to himself as an "intellectual thug," fully prepared to hit all and sundry over the head with his "percepts" – *not precepts!* – "outerings," and "probes," but he's no longer interested in literary criticism to accomplish this, confesses he, especially since it's clear to him (with the failure of his first book) that literary criticism will do little to advance his dream of making a difference in the world with the Great Book he knows he can and will write.

In short, he tells Pound he's made a major mistake settling on the study of English literature as a scholarly profession when really, all along, his primary concern has been to study technology and the way in which it affects both culture and the environment. He'd recently discovered this while reading the epic studies, *Empire and Communications* and *The Bias of Communications*, just published by his University of Toronto associate, Harold A. Innis (noted for the breadth and depth of his theoretical insights as much as his encyclopedic mind).

If you look at Innis's approach, states McLuhan, you discover the evidence supporting the assertion that phonetic writing transformed Greek civilization without that society having even the slightest notions of how it had happened. It is this pair of works by Innis, maintains McLuhan, that provides him with the extra edge he needs to successfully mount a full-scale investigation and exploration aimed squarely at understanding the social and psychological implications of technology and media in order to report objectively upon the effects of both.

Although he and Innis are constitutionally incapable of sustaining a friendship – Innis is a liberal thinker while McLuhan's deeply conservative – the ill-matched pair nevertheless manages to trade valuable information and ideas concerning the nature of art, media, technology, culture, and styles of communication, both oral and written.

McLuhan introduces Innis to Pound's "ideogrammic" book-writing method (which, in its condensed features and startling juxtapositions, loosely resembles those techniques traditionally employed by the Menippean satirists). For his part, Innis clarifies much for McLuhan when he reveals that, in oral intercourse the eye, ear, brain, human sensorium, and all related faculties "act together in busy cooperation and rivalry, each eliciting, stimulating, and supplementing the other."

∞

In the midst of all this, Idea Consultants is born. A partnership venture among five principals – the McLuhans, William and Corinne Hagon, and Murray Paulin – its business is to sell ideas of all kinds to every taker in any field of endeavour, from banking and advertising to corporations and institutions.

After almost two years of brainstorming sessions, Idea Consultants has dreamed up hundreds of innovative items (including semi-liquid soap in travel-size pouches, frozen diet dinners, soft drinks in aluminium cans, a transparent potty-training apparatus to eliminate the lift-and-check problem, lawn-mower headlights, bandages on an adhesive-tape type of dispenser called Peel-Aids, television platters [a.k.a. videocassettes] and, astonishingly, an idea for a real-time TV programme involving interactive problem-solving where the wily winner, by wit and cunning, takes the grand prize).

∞

The birth of the youngest McLuhan, Michael Charles (19 October 1952), combined with the many fresh and exhilarating ideas Innis has planted in the six-time papa's highly fertile brain, reinforce his resolve and concernitude to push ahead and make something of himself (for Corinne, their family, and the future).

∞

Edmund ("Ted") Carpenter, a close friend and esteemed colleague from the university's anthropology department he'd met in 1948, understands McLuhan's dilemma perfectly. Thus, when Carpenter hears that the Behavioural Sciences Division of the Ford Foundation in the United States is awarding a number of two-year interdisciplinary research grants in the amount of fifty thousand dollars for innovative projects that include seminars as part of their game plan, he suggests the possibility of the pair of them making a joint application, a suggestion McLuhan enthusiastically endorses.

"Come on, Ted, we'll win kudos from people we respect," urges the guy many on the campus have taken to referring to as a nut or charlatan, often within hearing range, "we've got it made here, there's so little talent."

∞

On 19 May 1953, the Ford Foundation announces the only successful group among the trio of applicants is the one headed up by Carpenter and McLuhan (who will shortly receive a research grant in the amount of $44,250).

Needless to say, the deliriously triumphant outcasts (as they've been called on more than one occasion), revel in the victory, especially when the university's president, Dr. Sidney Smith, writes the winners a congratulatory note expressing his respect and admiration for the accomplishment of a significant breakthrough insofar as McLuhan and Carpenter have become the first ever recipients of the Ford Foundation's investment in Canadian scholarship.

∞

McLuhan doesn't stop there nor, for that matter, does his salary. It increases to the point that St. Michael's Basilians feel confident enough to loan him the cash to invest in a home for his family at a very low rate of interest. It is a moment of delight, especially for McLuhan's ailing mother (who proudly crows Dr. McLuhan, the famous son she's nurtured, is now caring for her needs in a way Herb never could).

∞

The day the family moves to the spacious, slightly shabby, and thoroughly comfortable home at 29 Wells Hill Road in downtown Toronto's gloriously green Annex neighbourhood located mere steps from the campus, the McLuhans quietly revel in this not inconsiderable accomplishment.

Tonight, prior to the magnificent "welcome-to-our-world" feast his wife's prepared, McLuhan says grace with gusto. Following the sumptuous spread at the exquisitely set table laden with the family's finest china, silver, and crystal, McLuhan surveys the fruits of the couple's labours: Six healthy kids, one rambling yet charming Tudor-style home, and two adults who are still very much in love.

"Not bad for someone who failed grade six, eh?" McLuhan pauses, puffs grandly on his Montecristo cigar, and burps contentedly. "And, you know, I can just feel it: The best is yet to come."

∽

In many respects, McLuhan's thinking the best is yet to come certainly proves correct; however, in 1956, it is overshadowed by a stroke his mother suffers that leaves her partially paralyzed, unable to speak, and in need of round-the-clock caregivers.

McLuhan, attuned to even the slightest of his mother's sufferings and indiginities as a result of her general helplessness and loss of speech, oversees Elsie's admission to Our Lady of Mercy Hospital in Toronto. Once a day, every day until her death, he makes the time to take the long streetcar ride to visit her in the hospital. Some days, he reads detective stories to her; other days, mother and son sit together in the hospital's courtyard; and, when circumstances require it, McLuhan cheerfully trims the unsightly and embarrassing hairs that sprout on her chin.

∽

"California, here we come... Open up that golden gate..."

"Marshall, please. No singing. Not while I'm driving. Why not switch on the radio, see if you can't find something the kids enjoy, too?"

"Corinne, My Dear, please yourself. I'm already pleased as punch; so, there's no need to 'Marshall, please' me. Who'd a-thunk it? Little Marsy McLuhan, grade-six flunkie, hitting the road to teach a summer course for real cold hard Yankee cash in the sunny heart of Santa Barbara, California, with his six fantastic kids and his absolutely gorgeous wife in one heck of a beaut of a beast of a vehicle. God bless the assembly-line crew who turned out the best Dodge station wagon ever built. Hands, er... Windows down!"

"Good one, Dad! Not bad at all."

"Well, what'll be, Guys? Listening to the radio or hearing some more of *The Canterbury Tales*? You know, your mother and I met in California? It's kind of a homecoming for us, isn't it, Sweetheart? Eric? Oh, Ear Ache? Would you thanks and kindly please pass me one of those fine Canadian beers so I might celebrate that blessed event? *Oh, Mabel, Black Label...*"

"Okay, okay... The votes on the table. All in favour of the *Tales* say, 'Cool, Daddy-O'; and, all in favour of the radio say, 'Hot, Pops.'"

"Hot, Daddy-O."

"Cool, Pops."

☙

In August, eight tanned and healthy McLuhans climb back into the ancient station wagon and point Ol' Reliable in the direction of Fort Worth, Texas, relishing the prospect of reconnecting with various members of the lively and entertaining Lewis tribe. Later, before returning to Toronto, the family pays a visit to the Strohbachs in St. Louis where Addie, sarcastic as ever, remarks that Ol' Reliable looks like it just drove off the set of *The Grapes of Wrath*. The Strohbachs marvel the car's transported the McLuhans this far.

"That's one gawddawful clunker of a station wagon you've got there, Marsh."

"Ah, Addie, 'fess up. You're just jealous!"

6

I-N-F-O-R-M-A-T-I-O-N

The media are always bigger than the event.
— Marshall McLuhan

Just prior to his 1958 Keynote Address to the National Association of Educational Broadcasters (NAEB) in Omaha, Nebraska, having supplemented his usual steak-and-potatoes breakfast with a pair of poached eggs and thickly buttered brown-bread toast, the lean and long-legged figure waiting in the wings feels oddly exhilarated and strangely comfortable preparing to take the spotlight.

Red leather, yellow leather, red leather, yellow leather, red leather...

Canadian photographer John Reeves gives his seal of approval to
McLuhan's striking wardrobe.

Absent-mindedly plucking lint from his favourite tweed jacket, the forty-seven-year-old's memories flash back to the day he'd first worn it, in Cambridge, at least two decades ago, now. *Little did I know*, he thinks, *little did I know that my theories would reach so many people. Or, for that matter, that they'd offend so many others. Well, they just don't get it. Not quite; not yet.*

Amid the din, thanks to his acute sense of hearing, McLuhan recognizes the voice of NAEB President Harry Skornia addressing the influential members of one of the leading educational organizations in the world. Now, he's thanking and welcoming them... Omaha. *Tick.* Bellwether organization. *Tick.* Radical and right! *Tick.* And, this evening... great honour... immense pleasure... special Canadian guest... Dr. Herbert Marshall McLuhan!

Bingo!

"Good evening, Ladies and Gentlemen; thank you, Dr. Skornia. I have never met an audience I didn't lick!

"All media are extensions of some human faculty – psychic or physical.

"The mother tongue is propaganda.

"Rumours are the 'real thing.'

"The medium is never neutral.

"We are the primitives of an unknown culture.

"Some people use statistics as a drunk uses a lamppost – for support rather than illumination.

"A man all wrapped up in himself makes a small package.

"Many a good argument is ruined by some fool who knows what he is talking about.

"The short cut is the long way round.

"The future is not what it used to be; neither is the past.

"The trouble with a cheap specialized education is that you never stop paying for it.

"Diaper backwards spells repaid. Think about it.

"Only puny secrets need protection. Big discoveries are protected by public incredulity.

"History can be changed.

"Art is what you can get away with.

"Give more credit than you take.

"Communication is what people with nothing to say do to people who won't listen.

"You don't like those ideas? I got others!

"Excellent, excellent! I like an audience who knows how to laugh at me. But, five will get you ten, you won't be laughing at me once I tell you a little about what I've learned, this past decade, mucking about with the very things you've been telling your kids to avoid like the purple-people-eater plague. All the popular stuff, in other words. Comic books? We got 'em. Glossy mags? We got 'em. Richard Nixon? Who wants him?

"For your information, let me ask you a question: If I told you all media, which derive from a single medium; that is, if I told you all media, which are based on the medium of language, have effects on the human psyche quite distinct from the information they seemingly provide, would you call me an ambulance?

"All right, I'm an ambulance. Fine. In fact, I'm a siren... No, make that an anti-siren! Today, I'm here to warn you tomorrow's history; so, it's time to return to school *en masse*. All of you. All of us. And, now that I've established what we'll all being doing for the next few years, allow me to explain:

"Learning and teaching go hand-in-hand. Teachers never stop learning. Learners never stop teaching. That's key. That's education. That's the stuff that makes the world go twirly-whirly, right?

"Wrong. Today, the stuff that makes the world go round is I-N-F-O-R-M-A-T-I-O-N! Information! And, the processing and packaging of I-N-F-O-R-M-A-T-I-O-N is big business, huge bucks, and the only game in town. Ain't no two ways about it. Our age is the age of I-N-F-O-R-M-A-T-I-O-N; our business is the business of I-N-F-O-R-M-A-T-I-O-N; and, in order to spell out exactly what I mean, think about GM, just for a second.

Okay? In the time it just took you to think about GM, good ol' IBM just eclipsed it in business. And, for your information, you know what else? GE, that's what. Gee, eh? GE still hasn't figured out what it's doing in business, despite its claim to being the Bright-Idea Light-Bulb company.

"Quick! Somebody flip the switch! GE is *not* in the business of making light bulbs, not only, not anymore. Oh, no, not by a long jump shot.

"Now, don't shoot me, I'm just the messenger; but, GE is in the business of moving information. I-N-F-O-R-M-A-T-I-O-N! *Electric light is pure information.* The General Electric Company makes a considerable portion of its profits from electric light bulbs and lighting systems. It has not yet discovered that, quite as much as Ma Bell, that poor dame who still thinks she's in the business of making telephones, it is very much in the business of moving information. Light is information. Light is a medium. And, you know what that means, don'tcha?

"The medium is the message."

∞

It was not the first time McLuhan spoke those five unforgettable words. When he'd addressed a smaller group of Vancouver broadcasters several months earlier, he'd used exactly that sentence. Then, as now, it stunned its listeners into a bewildered silence tempered by genuine awe. Then, as now, it both makes perfect sense and yet, it perplexes. Endlessly. Not quite a paradox, not quite a simple and pat answer to an impossible question, the medium-message maxim does indeed make sense in context.

As he explains in 1964's *Understanding Media*, after "3,000 years of explosion by means of fragmentary and mechanical technologies, the Western world is imploding. During the mechanical ages we had extended our bodies in space. Today, after more than a century of electric technology, we have extended our central nervous system itself in a global embrace, abolishing both space and time as far as our planet is concerned. Rapidly, we approach the final phase of the extensions of man – the technological simulation of consciousness, when the creative process of knowing will be collectively and corporately extended to the whole of human society, much as we have already extended our senses and our nerves by the various media."

Is this, according to the good doctor, A Good Thing? McLuhan's not entirely sure: "Whether the extension of consciousness, so long sought by advertisers for specific products, will be 'a good thing' is a question that admits of a wide solution. There is little possibility of answering such questions about the extensions of man without considering all of them together. Any extension, whether of skin, hand, or foot, affects the whole psychic and social complex."

McLuhan assures audiences and readers, over and over, again and again, his five-word pronouncement speaks for itself, eloquently, when both its terms – "medium" and "message" – are properly understood.

By media, he elaborates, he does not simply mean information-packed magazines, newspapers, radios, televisions, and billboards; rather, he defines a medium (or a combination of media) as any extension of the body, brain, or being (including, of course, new technologies such as the computer). Clothing is an extension of skin; eyeglasses extend sight; a house extends the body's ability to keep itself warm; and, a bicycle or gas pedal extends the foot. McLuhan doesn't suggest content plays *no* role; rather, it plays a distinctly subordinate one. "By placing all the stress on content and practically none on the medium," notes he, "we lose all chance of perceiving and influencing the impact of new technologies on man."

The message of a medium is not the content it provides to the user or the audience of any medium; rather, the message of a medium exists in its ability to effect change or change a society or culture. Consider the different ways an individual can learn of the death of a celebrity, for example. There's speech (or gossip), there's the tabloid take (or gossip in print), there's TV footage of the details of the death including officials confirming the accuracy of the report; and, there's an obituary notice in a newspaper. The medium carrying the message makes as much difference as the message itself. It is one thing to hear or read the news that JFK has just been assassinated in Dallas, Texas; it is another thing entirely to view the well-known twenty-six-second Zapruder news clip on the tube, for example. In precisely this respect, the medium is indeed the message.

In McLuhan's view, a cool medium (telephone, cartoons, television, speech), a medium of low definition, is one which actively involves its user both emotionally and mentally because it's poorly defined and doesn't provide its user with a great deal to process (through the senses); thus, the user works harder to fill in the blanks and make sense of the medium. It demands *involvement*.

A hot medium (radio, photography, print, lectures), a medium of high-definition, is one which requires little participation from its user because it does much of its user's work; thus, its user doesn't need to become involved emotionally or mentally to fill in the blanks and make sense of the medium. It engenders *detachment*.

In experiments with involvement and participation, McLuhan and crew discovered, for example, that a class watching a television broadcast inviting them to join in a sing-along happily did so; but, when a movie was shown with the same entertainers inviting the same class to sing along with them, the class remained silent.

The essential difference, then, between high- and low-definition media is one of amount, quantity, or volume in terms of impact on the human psyche and the basic dynamics of the human sensorium by the media:

High-definition media (hot) are low in participation; low-definition media (cool) are high in participation (which does not refer to intellectual involvement; rather, participation refers to how much a medium engages our senses). The controversial aspects of McLuhan's views involve his certainty that it is neither the content nor the central ideas media disseminate that influence and shape society; rather, it is media which fulfil this function.

Before the invention of the medium of movies, reading a novel was an individual activity; after its invention, a movie made it possible for groups to collectively "view" a novel on a screen in a theatre near them. The change from an individual reading a novel at home to a group of people viewing it on screen in public is obvious, maintains McLuhan. Would hot-buttered popcorn be such a hit if it weren't a movie staple?

Additionally, media work in pairs; one medium always contains another (and that medium contains another and...). The medium of the movie contains the medium of the novel. The medium of the novel contains the medium of the printed word. The medium of the printed word contains the medium of writing. The medium of writing contains the medium of speech. There it ends since, of course, speech is pure process.

Following the resounding success of his presentation the night he announces to the world that the medium is the message and explains why it is so, McLuhan accepts a flattering offer from Harry Skornia (in his capacity as NAEB's president). In the fall of 1959, he goes on sabbatical to accept the role of the team leader working on a project to develop a syllabus for the study of media in grade eleven classes. The project, funded by the NAEB, allows McLuhan the time (and income) to investigate what he calls "the mutational powers" of a medium (and not that medium's content).

McLuhan hopes to teach the "grammar" of the new languages of television, radio, and related media. In doing so, he reiterates, he'll demonstrate the way in which media impose their own set of assumptions upon their users (or shape their users' perceptions, actions, and apprehensions). He considers it imperative the contemporary world truly understand the nature of media (particularly electronic media) and their effects upon society and culture.

Unlike previous technologies (which extend a single sense), the new media of electronic technologies extend the entire nervous system. The way information moves in such media corresponds to the way in which information moves in the human brain. It is only through a precise understanding of the implications of these new media, he warns, that traditional values of literacy and Western civilization will continue to flourish.

This is the substance of the analyses and recommendations in his "Report on Project in Understanding New Media" to the NAEB. As he states in its preface, the report will also provide the basis for the book he intends to write expounding upon the way in which media are capable of imposing their own assumptions on the people who use them.

In a note attached to the Report, McLuhan reveals his health has broken under the stress of prolonged overwork on the project. He's recently been released from hospital and his doctor insists he take a good long rest, advice a hospital-phobe such as McLuhan, he jokes, is inclined to follow. Ted Carpenter, McLuhan's long-time U of T friend and fellow Ford-Foundation researcher, confirms McLuhan did indeed suffer a stroke earlier that year, a stroke that caused such alarm his employer (and confessor) Father John Kelly was summoned to administer the Last Rites.

When McLuhan returns to teaching in the fall of 1960, however, he cavalierly pretends he never suffered a stroke. But his family and close friends can clearly see the toll it's taken: the man who was a robust and animated specimen has turned into an old man overnight. His nervous intensity's more pronounced. He's incapable of relaxing for more than five minutes at a stretch.

∞

On 10 July 1961, eleven days before his fiftieth birthday, McLuhan's mother passes away. Her death knocks him for a loop. When only a handful of mourners attends her funeral, his grief is compounded by that hurtful fact. Still, he gathers up her clothes and possessions, stores them in a closet in his room, and locks the door to the closet. Sometimes, he confides to close friends, he feels her ghost lives there still. He hears Elsie restlessly rustling among the gowns she proudly wore during the years she performed her dramatic monologues.

∞

That spring, *Explorations in Communications*, the anthology of articles collected from *Explorations*, the journal he'd founded with Mr. Dependable, Ted Carpenter, is readied for publication. That summer, driven by demons as much as dreams, McLuhan buries himself in the task of pulling together the manuscript for his follow-up to *The Mechanical Bride*. In it, he will focus on his studies of logic, rhetoric, and grammar as well as expanding upon his recent media discoveries so that he might present a more accurate appraisal of Western culture.

This, he vows, will be his Great Book, the one revealing the underlying laws of the total pattern, the one that will, among other things, show how the medium of print, the introduction of the printing press, and the growth of literacy, for example, profoundly affected every aspect of Western civilisation. And, no more moral earnestness. Not this time out. No sirree. It's oral boisterousness, noisy brashness, or bust. Oh, yeah.

McLuhan thanks his lucky stars for Corinne's intuitive grasp of his ideas and theories and her appreciation of the fertile muck, not to mention her intelligence in understanding all the nooks, angles, and crannies of his mosaic approach to style as well as the reason why he says he's not writing a book, he's packaging one readers can open and enjoy on any page. Will *this* volume be the one worthy of dedication to her?

In the spring of 1962, despite seemingly endless requests for interviews and commentaries from reporters, journalists, and businessmen, McLuhan delivers *The Gutenberg Galaxy: The Making of Typographic Man* to his editors at the University of Toronto Press. When it hits bookstores later that year, the reviews run the gamut:

The New Stateman's Alfred Alvarez calls attention to the author of "a lively, ingenious, but infinitely perverse *summa* by some medieval logician who has given up theology in favour of sociology and knows all about the techniques of modern advertising."

Encounter's Frank Kermode concludes McLuhan's book provides "a fresh and coherent account of the state of the modern mind in terms of a congenial myth. In a truly literate society, his book would start a long debate."

The Times Literary Supplement takes up the debate, inviting McLuhan to submit an article on the effects of print, an invitation that means more to him than all the other reviews combined. It represents one sweet vindication for everything he's certain he – *Mr. McLuhanatic! Marshwallow McLoonie!* – has communicated in *The Gutenberg Galaxy.*

McLuhan believes he's shown why the normal and natural tribal state of humanity in the Western world was demolished by the introduction of the phonetic alphabet. He additionally believes he's demonstrated the reason why the invention of print effected an even more radical transformation in the Western mind, a transformation that opened the portals of visually oriented reality favouring the trivium's branch of logic (over rhetoric and grammar) and leading to such phenomena as rationalism and nationalism, left-to-right reading, scientific and industrial development, and capitalistic consumerism. He knows he's proven the "new electronic interdependence recreates the world in the image of a global village."

And, in the final paragraph of *The Gutenberg Galaxy*, McLuhan lays it on the line:

"What will be the new configurations of mechanisms and of literacy as these older forms of perception and judgment are interpenetrated by the new electronic age? The new electric galaxy of events has already moved deeply into the Gutenberg galaxy. Even without collision, such coexistence of technologies and awareness brings trauma and tension to every living person. Our most ordinary and conventional attitudes seem suddenly twisted into gargoyles and grotesques. Familiar institutions and associations seem at times menacing and malignant. These multiple transformations, which are the normal consequence of introducing new media into any society whatever, need special study and will be the subject of another volume on understanding media in the world of our time."

Naturally, following the Governor General's Awards gala held in Ottawa (where he accepts the medal for 1962's best work of critical prose), McLuhan's convinced he's right, especially in that instant when he beholds his gracious, elegant, and ravishing wife making herself comfortable in the limousine and announcing in dulcet tones redolent of the mystique of the deep south, that she just loves Canada.

Stogey in hand, the southpaw holds court during his famed weekly seminars at the University of Toronto.

7

The Centre of the University

Radical changes in identity, happening suddenly
and in very brief intervals of time, have proved
more deadly and destructive of human values
than wars fought with hardware weapons.
— Marshall McLuhan

Whether as a counter-reaction to the dismissive
snubbery of all but a handful of his university
colleagues, or the realization of his long-cherished
dream to form a community of like-minded intellects,
or simply the guy's boundless love of talk for its own
sake – season in and season out – McLuhan holds
informal gab-sessions and seminars at both his office
and home.

Sometimes, he invites one of his classes to the house for a session. Nothing pleases him more than reading poetry aloud or hearing it read aloud while clustered around the living-room hearth. Invariably, Corinne sends everyone on their way with a cup of hot cocoa.

Attended by various friends, family members, disciples, voyeurs, acolytes, proselytizers, and even the occasional argumentative dissenter, the reputation of these spirited weekly gatherings of McLuhanitics practising *mcluhanisme* snowballs to the point long-haul friend and University of Toronto president, Claude Bissell, finally relents.

Mac shall have his centre.

McLuhan's boss at St. Mike's, Father John Kelly, applauds the president's smartuitiveness. Several universities south of the border are trying to woo him "with two, three, five times as much money," he tells the president. The president doesn't doubt it; but, he ruefully notes, many of Mac's colleagues would probably help him pack.

"Heh," quips Father Kelly, "sour gripes!"

"Dear Lord," replies the president, "not you, too, Father!"

∽

In 1963, Dr. McLuhan is appointed inaugural director of the University of Toronto's Centre for Culture and Technology for purposes of investigating "the psychic and social consequences of all technologies" as well as creating a dialogue among the university's many departments, faculties, and students. He's released from at least half his normal teaching duties and his interdisciplinary-research centre, a dilapidated red-brick schoolhouse at 96 St. Joseph Street on St. Mike's campus with its cracked windows and creaky wooden floors, prepares to open its ill-fitting front door to the world.

Soon, the centre holds stacks of six- to seven-thousand books, a couple of dozen folding chairs, and an ancient chaise longue (where McLuhan takes his half-dozen daily catnaps), all presided over by a Crucifix, the director's Cambridge rowing oar, and his freshly mimeographed copy of the Culture & Technology course description from the calendar of the School of Graduate Studies:

"Media and Society/A course considering media as man-made environments. These environments act both as services and disservices, shaping the awareness of users. These active environments have the inclusive character of mythic forms and perform as hidden *grounds* of all activities. The course trains perception of the nature and effects of these ever-changing structures."

As students promptly discover – like the words *medium, message, participation,* and *involvement* as McLuhan defines them – the words *figure* and *ground* possess a meaning all their own. "Unless you see figure and ground simultaneously," he's fond of saying, "you don't have the whole picture."

According to McLuhan, "nothing has its meaning alone. Every *figure* must have its *ground* or environment. A single word, divorced from its linguistic ground, would be useless. A note in isolation is not music." In simple terms, a person absorbs and processes information about a figure (an object, element of a structure, or situation) – say, a balaclava – in its context, environment, or ground.

A photograph of an Arctic explorer wearing a balaclava doesn't elicit the same response as a photograph of a bank robber wearing a balaclava. Normally, when an object or structure seems logical, its ground "disappears" and usually escapes notice.

In order to understand "the whole picture" of any situation or structure, it's essential to see both its figure and ground simultaneously (which bears a direct relationship to McLuhan's ideas concerning composition and style in his own writing).

∞

McLuhan agrees to take a relaxing and long-overdue working vacation where he earns five-hundred dollars a day discussing media and technology while cruising the Aegean with luminaries such as anthropologist Margaret Mead and architect, engineer, mathematician, and cosmologist Buckminster "Spaceship Earth" Fuller. It's a well-publicized event, a floating think-tank session with much to share with the world concerning culture, technology, anthropology, and ecology. Afterwards, the tanned and refreshed fifty-three-year-old darling of the media returns to Toronto to take up his work at the Centre with several brilliant ideas busily burning holes in the various pockets of his brain.

∽

If all goes smoothly in the professional and public spheres, the situation on the homefront is not quite so rosy.

By any account, McLuhan is not a model father in the departments of attention and demonstrative affection. A workaholic if ever there was one, he devotes much of his time and invests most of his energy to preparing and polishing his projects, presentations, speeches, and media appearances.

By all accounts, the prototypical Alpha male tends to take his wife (also known as the chauffeur, the budget-banker, the typist, the cook, the housekeeper, the attentive mother, the gracious hostess, the loving woman, and the valued confidant) for granted. As much as he loves his family, it takes a backseat to both his religion and his career. His wife fortifies and sustains him. His six children frequently confound and perplex him.

He's flabbergasted, for example, when one of his daughters refuses to say the Rosary following the evening meal. He's further knocked off his spots by Michael, the youngest McLuhan. He casts about for reasons to explain his youngest's increasing aversion to the Catholic faith.

But, it's 1964. The civil rights movement is in high gear. The conflict in Southeast Asia is growing. The Beatles dominate the pop charts; Ed Sullivan dominates Sunday-night variety TV; and, the McLuhans enjoy watching *Perry Mason, I Spy, Hogan's Heroes, Wayne & Shuster, The Man from U.N.C.L.E., Gilligan's*

Island, and *Dr. Kildare* together. Plus, every once in a while, the family takes a leisurely tour of the city in that recently acquired brand-new Ford, which understandably pleases Madame McLuhan a great deal.

It's well and good, thinks she, to vent about such expensive servomechanisms (mechanical slave-makers) as automobiles; but, when her husband needs to go somewhere in a hurry – and, when doesn't he? – he's the first one to strap himself into that good ol' servomechanism.

It's 1964 and McGraw-Hill's readying McLuhan's most ambitious work, *Understanding Media: The Extensions of Man*, for publication. Basically a rewrite and elaboration of the NAEB Report (his wife retypes three times), *Understanding Media* explores the way in which electr(on)ic media reflect and influence modern civilization:

"Today," writes McLuhan in its introduction, "after more than a century of electric technology, we have extended our central nervous system in a global embrace, abolishing both space and time as far as our planet is concerned."

Understanding Media, resembling a traditional book not at all, sells 100,000 copies within weeks of its arrival in bookstores throughout the Western world. True, it contains an introduction, seven chapters discussing media in general, and twenty-six chapters discussing specific media (such as speech, clocks, money, television, the automobile, movies, newspapers, light, etc.).

In its first chapter, "The Medium Is the Message," McLuhan restates his basic premise: Media are capable of imposing their own assumptions on those who use them. Later, he clarifies himself, stating that each new medium creates its own environment which acts on human sensibilities (the human sensorium) in a "total and ruthless" fashion. A new medium does not simply add itself to what already exists; rather, it affects or transforms what already has existed (through such phenomena as extension, displacement, amputation, cannibalization, and anesthetization).

A movie, for example, doesn't exist in a vacuum. Because of the medium of movies, drive-ins, movie theatres, screens, projectors, trailers, concession stands, parking lots, and posters, to mention but a few, also come into existence. (And, of course, a movie contains the medium of the novel.)

Understanding Media is not a book that begins at the beginning and ends at the end, a fact McLuhan stresses repeatedly, pointing out that he encourages a dip-and-dive approach to his mosaic – or collage-like collection of probes, observations, and assertions. To make his points, he shamelessly admits, he prods, pokes, fudges facts, spouts aphorisms (or what he calls verbal hand grenades), spews wisecracks, and stops at nothing to illuminate his views (including several controversial ones where he makes it clear he opposes birth control, pro-choice abortion, pornography, feminism, homosexuality, sex education, non-white immigration, Masonic secret societies, Marxism, Communism, and the Second Vatican Council, a.k.a. Vatican II).

Strongly affected by the full moon, which he firmly believes causes many of his misfortunes, the highly superstitious McLuhan's something of an amateur numerologist (a fact which provides the McLuhanacy mockers with further evidence of his chicanery and charlatanism). McLuhan approves of the idea that his thirty-three chapters will put readers in mind of the death and resurrection of Christ. He purposely ensures the chapters devoted to discussing individual media equal the number of letters in the alphabet, a sly way for the wily wordsmith to communicate the importance he attaches to that medium, that most important medium, the one which affects all Western technologies following in its wake. As twenty-six letters go, so goes civilization.

McLuhan elaborates upon media hot and cold as well as "the extensions of man" in the book, expanding upon the idea that every human artefact is an extension of either one of the five senses (among the human sensorium) or a part of the body. He shows the hateful ways in which such artefacts reduce humans to being nothing more than the sum of their servomechanistic parts in a world where taste is dictated, selection confined, and lowest-common-denominator dynamics proliferate and dominate (while authentic wants, needs, and desires are chronically delayed, denied, derided, or destroyed) in the name of organized dissatisfaction.

When turned into a servomechanism of say, an automobile, the foot of the individual can no longer perform its primary or basic function of walking; true, the individual can indeed cover great distances quickly; but, in effect, the individual is paralyzed and immobilized.

In this respect, technologies and media both extend and amputate basic human functions and social structures. Amplification becomes amputation. Electr(on)ic media create a virtual explosion of human activity, of extension and amputation and extension and amputation (or expansion and collapse...).

∞

As far as McLuhan's concerned, artists are what his pen pal Ezra Pound calls "the antennae of the race." Or, as his old friend from his Windsor days, Wyndham Lewis, avers, the artist is the only individual "engaged in writing a detailed history of the future" because the artist "is the only person who lives in the present." Only the artist is capable of accurately sizing up the present, of see(r)ing it. That's part of what makes an artist an artist, is it not?

Artists, in McLuhan's view, function rather like an advance-warning system alerting their society to the effects of new media. In this respect, it becomes clear McLuhan is himself an artist, an explorer, a sleuth of the everyday for the benefit of every tomorrow.

It comes as no surprise his favourite quote – "We were the first that ever burst/ Into that silent sea." – issues from S. T. Coleridge's horror-laced poem, "The Rime of the Ancient Mariner."

∞

It similarly comes as no surprise *Understanding Media* earns praise and vilification in equal measure. *The New Yorker's* Harold Rosenberg sniffs that the book's author "regards most of what is going on today as highly desirable, all of it meaningful," and cites claims such as McLuhan's contention the computer will link minds together to create a kind of network consciousness to prove his point:

"Today computers hold out the promise of a means of instant translation of any code or language into any other code or language. The computer, in short, promises by technology a Pentecostal condition of universal understanding and unity."

"*Pfft*," responds McLuhan, "this man can't read! I tell readers what a computer *promises* to do and all of a sudden, I love the idea and consider it highly desirable? Listen, because I can see a day where we'll be toting portable computers about the size of hearing aids so we're all wired, intermeshed, and connected in the great global consciousness, because I envision this great interconnected electronic grid, I personally think this is A Good Thing?

"Look, I'm just the messenger. I would think the features of the new media I've outlined would inspire sufficient revulsion in anyone within earshot to avoid them like the plagues they're about to become. *I'm not a crusader, I'm an investigator... The explorer is inconsistent. He must be... I don't prescribe. I merely wish to understand the power of these new forms in order to avoid them!*"

∞

McLuhan becomes a household name (as well as a snark-bite synonym for nonsensical chicanery), thanks partially to a pair of awe-inspired "genius scouters" who take on the English professor's promotion duties with exhilarating enthusiasm. Soon, *Harper's* dubs McLuhan "Canada's intellectual comet." *Fortune* describes him as "one of the major intellectual influences of our time." Not to be outdone, *The New York Times* designates him "the number-one prophet" of the consciousness-expanding age of art. To top it all off, one of the genius scouters creates fifty-thousand bumper stickers posing the question and seeking the answer the entire global village wants and needs to know:

WATCHA DOIN MARSHALL McLUHAN?

At this moment, he's attending a particularly memorable media meet-and-greet involving his introduction to quip-lash journalist and novelist Tom Wolfe. The intrepid Wolfe sets about crafting an incisive portrait of the universally revered probe-maestro in a much-quoted article for *New York* magazine, at one point even flying to Toronto to observe the poet of possibilities, "the artist" in residence, so to speak.

At the same time, American critic Gerald E. Stearn, in his just-published collection of essays, *McLuhan Hot and Cold*, opines "[McLuhan] can only be considered a stimulating thinker on a scale quite similar to Freud and Einstein."

It is here, in his essay included in Stearn's *McLuhan Hot and Cold*, Wolfe delights in describing the maestro of the miraculous at work, observing with some bemusement that McLuhan "sits in a little office off on the edge of the University of Toronto that looks like the receiving bin of a second-hand bookstore, *grading papers*, grading papers, for days on end, wearing – well, he doesn't seem to care what he wears. If he feels like it, he just puts on the old striped tie with the plastic neck band. You just snap the plastic band around your neck and there the tie is, hanging down and ready to go!"

Neither a fan of fashion nor of clothes, for that matter, McLuhan's wardrobe, such as it is, consists of three suits (a seersucker, a sporty plaid, and a traditional business outfit) and a wild and wicked collection of psychedelic ties (mostly of the clip-on variety). The comfort-lover favours casual slacks, cowboy boots, and ten-gallon hats.

Even during prosperous times, the Depression-raised McLuhan finds it difficult to spend on himself; but, he hints heavily Santa could land in his good books should she remember his great fondness for Hawaiian shirts.

Following a chi-chi luncheon in New York where McLuhan delights in wearing his favourite tweed jacket, Wolfe howls heartily: "He was a serious-faced Lewis Carroll... Nobody knew what the hell he was saying. I was seated at a table with a number of people from Time-Life, Inc. Several of them were utterly outraged by the performance. They sighed, rolled their eyeballs, and began conversing among themselves as he spoke..."

In the Sunday magazine of *The New York Herald Tribune*, Wolfe subsequently wonders, "Suppose

McLuhan is what he sounds like, *the* most important thinker since Newton, Darwin, Freud, Einstein, and Pavlov – what if he is right?"

To which, McLuhan, with his trademark Gary-Cooper smile replied, "I'd rather be wrong."

∞

By the time cartoons featuring McLuhan begin appearing in the pages of *The New Yorker*, the era's premier theorist of mass communications, its leading lecturer to the world entering the global village, is frequently designated a prophet or visionary.

∞

During the summer of Canada's centenary celebrations, several prominent Liberals under then-Prime Minister Lester B. Pearson enlist the services of the oracular opinionist for an informal series of brainstorming chat sessions.

Although non-partisan (with an aversion to Marxism), McLuhan acknowledges "the ultimate effect of new media is to make us all conservatives" and politics "offers yesterday's answers to today's questions." However, he shudders to think of the damages megacorporations wreak, fully endorsed by whomever happens to be holding the reins of power.

Besides, he sees politics as nothing more than a division of entertainment, noting that modern statespersons have become only too happy to abdicate their essential selves while their images substitute style for substance; after all, an image is much more powerful than a mere mortal could ever hope to be. McLuhan believes TV will prompt politicians to become entertainers as style and image dwarf substance and "the news" becomes just another package of entertainment. He ruefully observes that "a four-year stint in the White House is no longer easily distinguishable from something arranged by a booking agency." Furthermore, given the direction of show-biz politics, an actor could very well become president within two decades. (Ronald Reagan moved into the Oval Office in 1980.)

McLuhan also foresees the huge social shifts TV advertising will produce and describes advertising as "a service industry that provides its satisfactions quite independent of the product," adding that viewers "are increasingly tending to get their satisfactions from the ad rather than the product." Advertisers, in fact, will learn much from McLuhan and forge new vistas using the medium in ways congenial to it. One of his canniest predictions, for example, would involve fifteen- and thirty-second commercials that actively simulate and demonstrate the accelerated quality of bombardment from all sides. McLuhan's text-image mosaic style will come to dominate both televisual and virtual reality since it's a given it doesn't take a linear plot to create certain effects when kicky irreverence and quick-cut collage techniques pioneered by McLuhan will turn the pyrotechnic trick far more effectively.

Naturally, the prognosticator's disinclined to take any of it very seriously:

"Me? Personally? I'm neither pessimist nor optimist… I'm an apocalyptic!"

⚭

The lively Liberal bull gabs grow into festive affairs staged in hotel suites and private clubs. At one such, while the brilliant elocutionist is holding forth on various features of acoustic and visual space, he hesitates. His eyes glaze over for several seconds. He shakes his head, blinks and re-blinks his eyes, and tries to pick up the thread of his point. A few minutes later, it happens again. Then, again. McLuhan excuses himself and heads for the bathroom.

(Apparently, he suffers from a mild form of epilepsy or, at least, that's the general consensus. He refuses to undergo tests. Tests equal hospitals equal a fate worse than death. *TNT!*)

Thud.

His co-bullers open the door. McLuhan's crumpled on the floor. He's unconsciousness. *Water!*

When he regains cosciousness, McLuhan urges his friends to take him home; he has no desire whatsoever to visit a hospital, thank you very much.

As the 1960s progress, the blackouts increase. McLuhan stubbornly ignores them. He's got at least six major projects on the front burner at the Centre and from forty to fifty lectures, speaking engagements, or interviews (with *Fortune, Life, Esquire, Harper's,* etc.) lined up for the coming year. He's got his course, his weekly seminar, his articles for *TV Guide, McCall's, Family Circle, Glamour, Look, Vogue, The Saturday Evening Post, Mademoiselle, Playboy*...

And then, there's his family (although, with the terrifying recurrence of the intensifying blackouts and the incredible demands on his time, life on the domestic front presents its own set of complications). No matter. Tests are out of the question. Hospitalization's out of the question. *Carpe carpus!* Case closed.

∽

The Centre hires McLuhan's first and only full-time secretary, Margaret Stewart, in 1963: She and her husband, Jim, are friends of Mac's. In 1964, she's officially appointed Secretary of the Centre for Culture and Technology or, as she says, she becomes McLuhan's Official Secretary.

It is said much of McLuhan's success in the world can be attributed first to his wife and his eldest son, Eric; then, next, to his personal secretary. She possesses an extraordinary ability to organize the jam-crammed life of her "testy" but "kindly" boss and his prolific output.

An invaluable asset to the director she reveres, Stewart runs the affairs of the Centre as well as taking dictation and typing McLuhan's endless correspondence, lectures, articles, speeches, and book manuscripts. Working alongside him, she silently corrects his grammar (much as his wife had) and often forces him to clarify a tangled utterance so that, on the whole, he makes as much sense as possible, under the circumstances.

Under the circumstances, McLuhan's devoted fans increase in numbers and visibility. Journalists, entertainers, politicians, advertisers, business folks, academics, and cultural revolutionaries including

Glenn Gould, Abbie Hoffman, John Lennon, Philip Marchand, Thomas Dilworth, Susan Sontag, Norman Mailer, Peter Goddard, Woody Allen, Timothy Leary, Peter C. Newman, and the Smothers Brothers number among his many high-profile, influential, and enthusiastic supporters.

But, under the circumstances, with the pressures of his public life steadily proving more time-consuming, his family life, already seriously strained, threatens to implode.

The twenty-one-year-old twins, Teri and Mary, have left home. Teri's gone off to Ottawa to study while spending her spare time working with the Company of Young Canadians. Mary's landed a plum job as secretary to the dean of the Golden Gate University Law School in San Francisco; she's spending summers at Lake Tahoe and attending New Year's Eve parties with Ol' Blue Eyes, Frank Sinatra.

The couple's children, now ranging in age from fourteen to twenty-four, remain a mystery to their father, particularly the youngest, who, it seems, is a true child of TV, right down to the fact he was born around the same time the Canadian Broadcasting Corporation began beaming its signal across the country for the first time. McLuhan worries for him. Already under the spell of the flower-power politics prevalent at the time, his youngest son is turning away from the Church, burning incense, reading Herman Hesse, and spouting Buddhist philosophy.

What next?

His gorgeous daughters (who take after their mother, naturally), are entering beauty contests.

Beauty contests! Flashing radiant smiles, winning prizes, parading on stages with all the savvy sophistication of Rita Hayworth.

When one or the other of his beautiful girls brings a beau to Wells Hill Road to meet the folks, McLuhan invites the nervous date to join him in the living room where he's stretched out on the floor in front of the fire and ready to talk. Most of the tongue-tied young men are more than ready to listen.

Eric, home following a three-year stint with the U.S. Air Force and enrolled at the University of Toronto, becomes his father's paid assistant responsible for various additional duties (including taking over much of the driving which frees up even more of his mother's time after her husband additionally hires an accountant to manage his burgeoning financial affairs and relieves her of the need to fulfil the role of bookkeeper).

Absolutely mad about James Joyce's *Finnegans Wake* (much to the delight of his dad), Eric assists his father preparing the manuscript for *The Medium Is the Massage: An Inventory of Effects* (a co-write/collaboration with Quentin Fiore and Jerome Agel which sells nearly a million copies when it is published in March 1967).

∞

In April 1967, McLuhan attends a San Francisco "happening," an afternoon peace rally at the panhandle of Golden Gate Park where wildly dressed, high-on-life, peace-loving hippies, draped in beads and bedecked with flowers, converge.

"There is no question," McLuhan remarks, "that this is a result of the new tribalism of the Electric Age…"

"Whether I can deal with it is another question."

McLuhan, in a contemplative mood, unwinds with a cigar.

8

Wise Guy to the World

In the global village, how stupid to celebrate
Mass in the vernacular!

– Marshall McLuhan

John Culkin, S. J., director of the Center for
Communications at New York's Fordham University,
wants to establish a research council – a media-and-
communications think tank – with McLuhan as its
leader.

*McLuhan doesn't. He can't bear the thought of
uprooting his family, overturning his comfortable routine, and leaving his reassuring Annex neighbourhood.
He's deeply attached to its lovely leafy streets, its close
proximity to the Centre with St. Basil's daily Midday*

Mass on campus, with Holy Rosary nearby for Sunday services. He's come to call it home, blah-blah-blah...

Culkin ups the ante: *Hrm-m.* The New York State Board of Regents has just approved his nomination for a Schweitzer Chair at Fordham University for one year, does he know?

He knows. Very nice; very flattering; but, with a list of achievements, citations, prestigious awards, and honorary degrees he's recently received from several universities – Assumption, Manitoba, Simon Fraser, Windsor, Iowa's Grinnell, and New York's Niagara among them – already under his belt, that's already quite the roster. No?

Impressive? Well, yes, of course, it's very impressive, very impressive, yes indeedee; but, the Schweitzer comes with an equally impressive hundred grand attached to it. Plus, a lovely house in Bronxville, in an equally idyllic neighbourhood, just far enough from the city core to be both comfortable and accessible to all the sites and spectacles the greatest city in the world offers.

You don't say? Nice tidy sum, too, considering most professors in our neck of the world earn about fourteen thou. Still, as much as Mac's disillusioned with colleagues who've been "asleep for at least five-hundred years" (and as much as he laments the cultural and literary wasteland he sees everywhere around him, from the "Canadian who is mildewed with caution" to Canadian writers, "a fifth-rate bunch of people who are very happy, very smug about themselves"), he reiterates he's perfectly happy living where he's living and doing what he's doing. He is, after all, fifty-five, eh?

Young Elizabeth starts university this fall. McLuhan's no doubt heard word she's been offered a scholarship from Fordham's new women's college, right?

Yup, right. Mac knows.

Then, he also knows about a pair of lifelong friends and trusted collaborators, namely, Harley Parker and your good self, coming aboard as part of the research team? And, he knows about Eric, as well, then? It'll almost be like home.

Almost...

Culkin casually drops his trump card on the table: Mac realizes, doesn't he, that Corinne very much wants to go? There's nothing she'd love more than to spend a year in New York with most of her family. He's talked this over with Corinne, right?

Wrong.

Turns out *that* was something the Know-It-All didn't know.

∽

The McLuhans take up residence at 1015 Kimball Avenue in New York's residential Bronxville enclave on 1 September 1967. Both Elizabeth and Michael pursue their studies at Fordham University. Eric, cultural-anthropologist Ted Carpenter, artist-designer Harley Parker, and Professor McLuhan prepare the syllabus for Understanding Media, the course the Schweitzer Chairperson will teach.

The team rolls up its collective sleeves in preparation for several projects and presentations already

crowding the agenda, not to mention the constant ring-
ing of the telephone. *Most abused instrument of the
twentieth century*, The Grumpy One grumbles.

Two minutes! At most! Two minutes, he insists,
that's the maximum amount of time a person needs to
spend on that contraption. Two minutes, tops!

Br-r-r-n-n-g-g-g!

"Dr. McLuhan, here. How may I help you? You're
welcome. I would like to clarify this point for you, Mr.
Trollkind, but you are the reporter, are you not? *You*
ask your questions. *I* provide my answers.

"Ergo, when you asked your question about
miniskirts, I provided you with my answer about
miniskirts:

*"The miniskirt is the ultimate act of violence. As
our world moves from hardware to software, the
miniskirt is a major effort to reprogramme our sensory
lives in a tribal pattern of tactility and involvement.*

"I see no need to elaborate further. I don't pre-
tend to understand my theories; after all, my stuff is
very difficult. I simply report what I perceive. Good
day, Sir!

"Praise be! Good-rid bye-byes to another one,
hehehehe…"

"Good one, Dad!"

" Journalism is *roman collectif*. After two minutes,
they bore themselves. That was Tom Trollkind, from
The Future, hopelessly foundering in the miasma of
myopia, perpetually losing ground. What else is news?"

☏

Stationed in New York, Tony Schwartz, a virtuoso in the field of advertising's audio effects, seeks out McLuhan following an epiphany he experiences reading *Understanding Media*:

"I was playing the same ball game – commercials – as other people were playing; but, I was playing in a different ball field. They were playing in a print-oriented ball field and I was playing in an auditory-structured ball field. After reading McLuhan's book, I understood that. It was almost as if it had been a rainy cloudy day and my discovering this in his book just made it the clearest blue-sky day you could ever have."

Believing advertising people to be the only ones who take him seriously, McLuhan participates in dozens of Schwartz's "auditory perception" classes (which the teacher records on cassettes), often accompanied by Ted Carpenter, John Culkin, Harley Parker, and Eric. The tapes represent the most significant achievement of McLuhan's research team during his year at Fordham.

Enter entrepreneur Eugene Schwartz. (No relation to ad-whiz Tony.) He dreams up *The Dew-Line Newsletter* and installs Eric in a penthouse office atop 200 Madison Avenue to edit it (with a salary of $15,000 per annum).

At the same time, director Stanley Kubrick invites the McLuhans to a private screening of his soon-to-be-released film, *2001: A Space Odyssey*.

Ten minutes after the projector starts rolling, McLuhan makes leaving noises. Teri changes his mind. Halfway through the film, McLuhan makes snoring

noises; fortunately, the soundtrack muffles those
sufficiently. Nobody, save his mildly embarrassed
daughter, notices.

∽

The world notices when the sage of the electronic age
enters Manhattan's Columbia Presbyterian Hospital –
nestled between New York's Harlem and Hudson
Rivers not far from Broadway's glittering lights and
Madison Avenue's slogan-happy marketeers – for
twenty-three days just before Christmas in 1967.

Perhaps best known as a dream of a teaching hospital, Columbia Presbyterian nevertheless becomes
McLuhan's worst nightmare. It is here the terrified six-
footer will trust his sight, sanity, and life to neurosurgeon Dr. Lester A. Mount.

"Under the circumstances," deadpans the wise
guy, "I'm happy to report I'm still alive and well and
living…

"Well… Let's just say this: I'm happy to report I'm
alive and well and living life to the dullest."

McLuhan's visitors – his devoted wife of twenty-
eight years and close friend, John Culkin, among them
– crack up. The slightly slouched salt-and-pepper-
haired smart-aleck coughs self-consciously, grins mischievously, uncrosses and recrosses his pyjamaed legs,
tilts his large head quizzically, and surveys the smiling
faces assembled together in the mint-green observation
room as if to say, "Well? What did you expect? Sgt.
Pepper's Lonely Hearts Club Band? Cartwheels? A
trampoline?"

Given the spring-sprong nature of his life these past few weeks, a trampoline's not as far-fetched as it sounds.

If McLuhan's wife had failed to convince him of the absolute necessity for this drastic measure, if Culkin had not further laid it on the line in no uncertain terms and succeeded in getting it through his thick skull that McLuhan, without the operation, would most assuredly be blind and bouncing off rubber walls within four months, the rash and recklessly determined patient might well have checked himself out of Columbia Presbyterian a second time, so great is his aversion to sickness, doctors, hospitals, and pain.

Despite the graphic details he's heard concerning the tumour the size of a tennis ball at the base of his skull, despite everything he knows about the meningioma's deadly effects; and yes, even despite the undeniable reality that, without undergoing the procedure, he'll most certainly be both blind and insane – not to mention the fact he might well be shaking hands with his Maker in a very short time – McLuhan had torn off his hospital gown, retrieved his street clothes, and checked himself out of the hated hospital before the tests that would eventually save his life had even been completed.

At present somewhat becalmed yet filled with fear, McLuhan stoically does his utmost to put up a brave front, if only for the sake of Corinne and the kids. He jokes about the standard-issue hospital room and its various culinary "feasts," declaring the rather bland food the best plastic he's ever eaten.

He strolls the halls of the neurosurgery ward and takes comfort in the steady stream of family, friends, and well-wishers enlivening the drizzle-iced rain, sleet, and snow he all too frequently notices from his window overlooking New Jersey's Palisades Park and Union City on the far side of the Hudson. He regards the foreboding clusters of bleak November clouds hovering above the Fort Washington Bridge outside the picture window apprehensively, observing they'd ominously started gathering the day he was admitted and haven't budged.

"I hope," he jokes half-seriously, "they're not a sign of things to come; you know, sympathetic fallacy; but, if they are, they are. It's up to Him, now."

Now, a murmur of subdued approval echoes around the room. McLuhan crosses himself, briefly rests his head on his chest, and brings his huge hands together in silent prayer.

"Well, then, Father," McLuhan says softly to Culkin as the last of his visitors prepares to head home in order to catch a good night's rest (in case he's needed at the hospital over the course of the next few days), "I only have one question: Do you think Dr. Mount drinks?"

Culkin looks up from the task of snapping the buttons on his galoshes shut. "Well, now, Mac," he evenly replies, "you can rest assured on that score. Dr. Mount is definitely not a drinker. In fact, he's a model of sobriety, not to mention he's probably the greatest neurosurgeon in the world. Lots of experience. Tonnes of accomplishments. The undisputed leader in his chosen field... although..."

"… Although!?"

"Although? Well, I'll break it to you gently, Marsh: I wouldn't want to put any money on it; but, if I were a gambler, I'd be willing to ante up a dollar or two on the odds that Dr. Mount will be popping the cork on a bottle of champers when this one's history."

"When? What do you mean, Culkin, *when*? Surely, surely, you mean if… *if!*"

"No, my friend, no *ifs*, *ands*, nor doubts about it. Knowing you, knowing Dr. Mount, I most certainly do mean when."

"Well, then, *when*?"

"Probably around this time Saturday night. Oh, I'd say, maybe five-six hours after the operation starts; so, I'd hazard a guess Dr. Mount'll be clinking glasses with his highly competent staff no later than 6:00 PM, tops."

"Bottoms up," McLuhan half-heartedly jokes.

"Good one, Mac. Nice *punctuation*, Wise Guy."

"*Pfft!* Wise guy? I feel like anything but a wise guy right now. I feel downright dumb, if you must know. I don't know why I let Corinne talk me into returning to this place! Or, Carpenter! Or, you! What was I thinking? Or, more precisely, what wasn't I thinking?

"No offence, Father; but, I sure as hell don't feel like a wise guy at all, not right now. Oh, yeah. That's a true and verifiable fact.

"But, incidentally, you know, speaking of wise guys, I'm sure you do know, don't you, that the word *wise* is a derivative of *weid* which also relates to *guide*, *guise*, *wit*, *idol*, *vision*, *advice*, *clairvoyance*, *survey*, *idea*, *history*, and *penguin*?"

"Penguin? You're joking!"

"Me? The wise guys' wise guy? Highly unlikely. You know me, Culkie: I only joke when I'm serious."

∽

The deadly serious work of detaching and removing the shockingly large tumour commences the morning of 25 November. Hundreds of media inquiries deluge the hospital.

Eric, pacing in the waiting room, checks and rechecks the time. With him, McLuhan's best friend and confidant of seventeen years similarly tracks the agonizingly slow progress of hands on the oversized face of the wall clock. McLuhan's brood gathers around the telephone in the Bronxville home, waiting for what seems like a dozen forevers for the first of the regular calls Eric or Carpenter will make from the hospital, as arranged, to deliver hourly progress reports and relay the latest concerning the condition of the head of their very close-knit family.

It's the Saturday following American Thanksgiving. Dr. Mount has already cautioned the McLuhans the operation could be a long and arduous ordeal. It could, he'd warned, take most of that day. He has no way of knowing beforehand, however, so five hours is simply a reasonable guesstimate.

Five excruciating hours pass. It's 4:30 PM. But, when the doors of the operating theatre open, it's only to allow a second squad of nurses and assistants to enter and replace the fatigued original support staff. Five more hours pass. The theatre doors open a second time; then, an unprecedented third platoon takes its place alongside Dr. Mount.

By now, it's the wee hours of the following day. It's Sunday morning and still, the operation continues.

Eric paces. Carpenter prays. Eric prays. Carpenter paces. The pair paces and prays together. Huddled around the black rotary-dial telephone, the family keeps its vigil, sighing in unison each time the gravity of the news that the operation's still in progress hits home.

"No news is good news," Teri assures her mother. "No news is good news, I just know it!"

Dr. Mount, already well-known as an artist in his highly specialized field, takes his time pondering each move, meticulously toiling away, conducting what will later come to be known as the finest performance of his professional life.

Maintaining an even hand and unwavering eye, the surgeon carefully gauges each move with all the grace, skill, and precision only a surgeon of his reputation can bring to the task at hand.

Right off the top, the doctor knows he'll have to lift McLuhan's brain in order to get at the tumour. He knows, too, he'll have to be quick about it. It's understood he will, unavoidably, be forced to expose some of the cells on the brain's surface to the potentially devastating effects of oxygenation. His esteemed patient's faculties will, almost inevitably, sustain some degree of damage.

He's made this clear to the McLuhans from the outset; but, it's this particular brand of devastating damage – caused by the air affecting the surface of his brain – Dr. Mount seeks to minimize and contain. This, above all else, concerns him acutely.

Extraordinarily methodical, extremely cautious, thinking long and hard, mentally rehearsing every move to be made before he attempts to make it, measuring and again measuring every cut with precision, sometimes taking twenty minutes to decide where the next cut will come, the doctor painstakingly wields his scalpel with the utmost care.

Then, finally, at five o'clock on Sunday morning, a full eighteen arduous hours later, the doors of the operating theatre swing open one last time:

"It's over."

The surgeon smiles weakly yet triumphantly, relief and exhaustion clearly written all over his face. "The effects of the anesthetic still haven't worn off, but Marshall is going to be fine, just fine."

An hour later, when McLuhan squintily opens one eye and looks up at the clock on the recovery-room wall, he understandably assumes it's 6:00 PM of the same day he was wheeled into surgery.

Dr. Mount, still apprehensively tending to his patient, waits until McLuhan begins to stir. Now, his charge groggily opens both eyes and struggles, slowly but surely, to reclaim consciousness.

"Marshall? Marsh? Can you hear me? The operation's over. It's Sunday morning. It's still snowing. How are you feeling?"

"Feeling? Well… that really depends on how you would define 'feeling.'"

Dr. Mount and the third team of assistants and nurses cheer. Their long, delicious, and gratefully welcomed laughter echoes throughout the hushed halls of Columbia Presbyterian. News of the patient's astonishing comeback quickly makes the rounds. Ted and Eric share the good news with both Culkin and the family.

Usually, patients require several hours to regain consciousness, and during that time, they frequently experience hallucinations after such procedures. McLuhan's clear, coherent, and hilarious response following such a gruelling operation turns him into something of a hero in the eyes of the hospital's neurosurgical staff.

Later, when the perennial punster opines the operation's indeed taken a load off his mind, McLuhan cements his reputation as a genuine legend in his own time. Not only that, this particular legend, considered by many a genius's genius, is still clearly in possession of his particularly wicked sense of humour, which, as the world will learn soon enough, has not suffered in the slightest.

On Monday November 27, while media outlets around the globe celebrate the success of the laborious eighteen-hour ordeal to remove the tumour from the brain of the world's leading communications specialist, McLuhan is, as the numbing effects of the anesthetic wear off, quite frankly, feeling like death.

The pain, he later remarks, was virtually indescribable and pretty much unendurable. Filling in the blanks in his journal later, he hits upon a pair of words that vividly describes the way he felt post-trauma:

Ruddy gore.

That Monday morning, bathed in pain, he berates himself for allowing the operation to go ahead, threats of blindness and insanity notwithstanding.

Just prior to leaving the hospital, McLuhan further notes in his journal that the experience of the surgery, coupled with the magnitude of unimaginable pain he's endured, have confirmed for him, indelibly, not only that he is wholly dependent upon and exceedingly close to God, but also that most exploits are futile in a world human beings have made, a world reduced to a global village virtually ruled – make that virtually dictatorized – by the ubiquitous messages of the media of communications.

The pursuit of such foolishnesses, he writes, is about as absurd and repulsive as a "bouquet of roses… in a death camp."

In short, McLuhan views what he discovers concerning the emptiness of most human endeavours as the same kind of message underscoring his own work in media studies:

At bottom, he gloomily concludes, everything is simply a shabby illusion built from the ground up (or the ground down) on the blind hopes, unrealized expectations, and foiled dreams of millions of discarnate individuals unavoidably enmeshed in the ubiquitous media, their insidious messages of organized dissatisfaction, and the invidious methods combining both.

Still, when McLuhan bids farewell to Dr. Mount and the neurosurgical staff at Columbia Presbyterian, his condition (or outlook) improves sufficiently enough that he can say, a little more optimistically, the pain is finally "halfway bearable... *Almost.*"

Ever mindful and always respectful of the gift that life increasingly seems to him to be, McLuhan almost weeps the day he exits Columbia Presbyterian.

The family, faithful to its pre-surgery promise not to discuss specific nitty-gritty details of the procedure their father has survived, shields the celebrated patient from the unblinking glare of the media's prying eyes. Corinne and the children are determined to ensure McLuhan's Christmas that year will be a memorable, festive, and joyous occasion, one that lifts his spirits and hastens his recovery from the longest brain operation performed in the history of American medicine, a record McLuhan wasn't really all that thrilled, quite understandably, to possess (despite his measured admission, several months later, he simply couldn't imagine his life without it).

Nevertheless, his life, after the trauma of major brain surgery, is forever altered.

The effects of the operation, in fact, linger until his death a dozen or so years later. But, in the months immediately following the ordeal, it becomes increasingly obvious to friends, family, and colleagues that McLuhan has changed, not always for the better.

His exceptionally acute senses of smell and hearing become hypersensitively attuned. Several associates, not unkindly, remember friends describing McLuhan during that time as "one exposed and quivering nerve" who is variously fragile, tense, irritable and, on occasion, uncharacteristically demanding and irrational.

The many descriptions seem fitting, particularly following an operation such as the one McLuhan has survived. On more than one occasion, it is said, McLuhan grumbles to his wife that he feels like he's walking into a chemical factory each time he enters their kitchen, the smell of household cooking, cleaners, herbs, and spices so overwhelms his sensorium.

But, it is the noises – the random noises taken for granted as part and parcel of contemporary existence – that prove by far the most intolerable. Any scraping, booming, or clashing sound drives him up one wall and down another. Airplanes, flying over Bronxville, situated directly beneath the flight paths of one of New York's major airports, turn him into a whimpering mass.

As a matter of course and self-defence, after his first train trip post-surgery (the entire duration of which he keeps his fingers plugged in his ears), McLuhan takes to carrying cotton-batting to absorb vibrational shocks he finds too painful to bear; for that reason, at the height of their popularity, McLuhan resolutely refuses to ride in a convertible unless the top is up and the windows shut.

Sadly, McLuhan's most desirable and obvious professional assets, his unstoppable energy and photographic memory, are both irreversibly damaged by the surgery.

On the one hand, he immediately notices his memories from the year or so before the operation are, at best, murky and muddled and, at worst, completely erased. He discovers he can remember faces but not recall the names attached to them; or, he remember the names of this or that old friend but cannot, for the life of him, conjure up their corresponding mental images.

On the other hand, to further complicate post-op matters, McLuhan discovers that "several years of reading got rubbed out," a fact which means he's required to reread hundreds of books. To make up for lost time and missing memories, McLuhan purchases armloads of study aids and guides normally used to provide students with both plot summaries and basic themes of major literary works.

But, curiously, almost perversely, memories long forgotten vividly resurface: Soon after his surgery, for instance, McLuhan's delighted to rediscover his abiding passion for the songs of Harry Lauder, a Scottish tenor he'd worshipped during his youth but hadn't given a moment's thought in years.

Natch, despite the fact he himself openly brags he can't carry a tune in a suitcase, McLuhan feels compelled to sing along with Lauder with a passion and conviction that does not, to say the least, overly impress those closest to him during his spontaneous eruptions and impromptu performances.

Although it takes almost two years before he begins to feel anywhere near his old self, McLuhan's recovery amazes friends, family, physicians, and caregivers alike. Even then, he's reluctant to admit, even privately, his former degree of emotional resilience and intellectual brilliance has vanished. *Well*, thinks he, *the devil laughs when you make plans; but, God is in the details.*

Thank God for God.

The biggest wheel on campus takes five for fun and games.

9

You Mean My Fallacy Is All Wrong?

> When we went to the moon, we expected pho-
> tographs of craters. Instead, we got a picture of
> ourselves. Ego trip. Self love.
>   – Marshall McLuhan

Shortly after surgery, McLuhan's lifelong booster,
one-time University-of-Toronto president Claude
Bissell, now teaching at Harvard and residing with his
family in Cambridge, Massachusetts, invites the king of
communications for dinner and a good night's bull-
shootery, an offer he happily accepts; however, upon
his arrival, he remembers he's forgotten to bring a gift
for the hostess responsible for the elegant repast she's
prepared in his honour.

Mortified, he excuses himself, exits the house, and strides briskly towards the commercial section of the university town.

The Bissells wait. Patiently. Very patiently. An hour later, the hostess asks her husband if he thinks Marshall's gone... where? Home, perhaps? Mac, Bissell replies, isn't that kind of guy. That's why, he explains, he thinks it's time to investigate Mac's puzzling disappearance further and steps out in search of his guest.

∞

"A mystery has been committed," quips McLuhan, once Bissell discovers him at the intersection of Hope and Crossland Avenues, a huge bouquet of baby's breath and blood-red roses clasped firmly in his hands.

"A mystery has been committed," he reiterates, "and, your house is missing!"

∞

By the spring of 1968, with America witnessing mass protests, cities in flames, the grievous war in Vietnam, and brutal racial confrontations, McLuhan's more than ready to return to Canada, not necessarily because he experiences anything remotely resembling pangs of patriotism. His love-hate relationship with the country of his birth is as much the result of wounded pride as it is the result of a sense of incredulity he's not accepted for all he's done right (and forgiven for being who he is, even when he's wrong, not unlike any other mortal).

He's more than ready to return home because he believes he needs the familiarity of his long-established routine to fully resume his work and life, not to mention the pressing catch-up demands and contractual obligations made upon him following the operation that has obviously taken its toll on the soon-to-be fifty-seven-year-old dynamo.

To capitalize on the spectacular success of *The Medium Is the Massage*, McLuhan again joins forces with graphics-designer Quentin Fiore and book-coordinator Jerome Agel to produce its follow-up, *War and Peace in the Global Village*, published in September 1968.

Unlike its "cubist" predecessor, it offers no attention-grabbing medley-mixings of image, text, and typographical pyrotechnics. Instead, it contains wide-ranging reflections and ruminations concerning the disappearing identity of the contemporary individual under siege by all manner of new media.

Thus, when radical activist Abbie Hoffman (who's just co-founded the Yippies with Jerry Rubin) declares that "the Left is too much into Marx, not enough into McLuhan" while promoting his latest work, *Revolution for the Hell of It*, McLuhan writes Hoffman off as the creator of just another manifesto for the new tribalism.

McLuhan scorns anyone who celebrates embracing the new tribalism because, in his view, it will ultimately overtake humankind, as subtly and inexorably as breathing itself, whether humankind celebrates it or not. No one is immune to the effects of the electronic age.

McLuhan fares slightly better with LSDeist Timothy Leary. Following their get-to-get, Leary comments McLuhan doesn't need to take LSD since he's already high on the yoga of his art form, talk.

"He talks in circles, and spirals, and flower forms, and mandala forms," the intensely awed pop-cult priest of psychedelia enthusiastically gushes. (Incidentally, McLuhan did mention, once, he'd be open to experimenting with the drug in a properly controlled environment; but, a friend dissuaded him on medical grounds.)

Later that year, flush from picking up the Canada Council's Molson Award for outstanding achievement in the Social Sciences, McLuhan's pleased to see *Through the Vanishing Point: Space in Poetry and Painting* in print. It's a labour of love based on long and exhilarating discussions concerning art and the human sensorium he and Harley Parker had first started writing during the 1950s.

Using extensive examples from poetry and painting, the authors examine issues of space, time, perspective, and interval from various angles. According to McLuhan, who is fond of reminding audiences and readers that "the action is in the interval," new media always alter the individual's sense ratio or the relationship among the five senses (of the human sensorium). New media, in effect, break the tyranny of print culture's emphasis on rational thought, linear logic, and left-to-right reasoning.

McLuhan ranks the five senses according to their ability to process the richness of the information transmitted to them. Sight's definitely the ace in the hole, the most complicated of the five, the one that allows perceptions of vast complexity as well as the processing of huge quantities of information.

If sight's the ace, then touch is the queen and hearing's the king. (Incidentally, if you close your eyes and then "look" at what's in back of you, you'll find yourself in what McLuhan calls acoustic space.) Smell and taste? Well, they make a great pair of boosts to sight (the visual), hearing (the acoustic or auditory), and touch (the tactile).

Again, in the example of the medium of film, the introduction of talkies altered the human sensorium of perception when Vaudeville – which appeals primarily to the visual, acoustic, and tactile – was supplanted by a medium for the masses or, more accurately, the malltitudes.

Although new media possess the potential to restore richer and more rewarding sensory balances among human beings, a fact counter-culturalists of the Woodstock generation (Hoffman, Leary, Lennon, Rubin, et.al.) find exceedingly agreeable, McLuhan's not all that sure such technological advances are worthy of the praise they seem to generate, almost effortlessly, of their own volition.

Have you heard the latest? The videophone will be a reality sooner than you can think to blink. If such a device does become popular, it will turn the global village into one ginormous theatre where traditional boundaries separating business, entertainment, and education will dissolve among themselves. This, in turn, will further accelerate the loss of individuals' authentic identities (as each is forced to play yet another specialized role, that of the video star).

∽

When McLuhan returns to Toronto, he is greeted with nothing less than complete and utter chaos ominously exhibiting signs of turning into a Pandemonium of anarchic confusement. Not only have the McLuhans decided the baronial house for sale just north of Toronto's Casa Loma in Toronto's Wychwood Park – all burnished oak panelling, airy rooms, high ceilings, and magnificent fireplaces – is the must-own home of their dreams, but, during his year-long absence, the university administration has elected to move McLuhan's Centre for Culture and Technology from its office at 96 St. Joseph Street to an ancient coach house beside St. Michael's Library tucked in back of a row of Victorian houses at the end of a lane off that same street.

Built in 1828, the rickety two-storey structure at 39 Queen's Park Crescent houses a seminar room with nineteen folding chairs as well as upstairs offices for McLuhan, his secretary, and a pair of university-paid assistants (his younger brother, Maurice "Red" McLuhan, and his long-time friendly sparring partner, artist Harley Parker).

No furniture worth noting. His library's arranged in great heaping stacks of books and magazines scattered holus-bolus on all available floor space throughout the dwelling (including the washroom where McLuhan's idea of smart decor consists of clippings of cartoons tacked to its water-stained walls). The leaded windows allow for a clear view of the splashes of dappled light on the ugliest green floor McLuhan's ever seen. It's got to go. He can't stand it. It's... it's... positively pukifying!

Wait a minute, urges his friend, abstract-artist René Cera, *this green is perfect, just perfect. This is the*

*queen of green, the kingpin colour for the work I plan
to create on that wall. Right there... Hold on. I've got
it! I can see it! I'll call it* The Pied Piper. *It will cover
the entire wall, from its ugly green floor to its pock-
marked ceiling. Just picture it! A great whirling semi-
chaosmotic mural, a wildly splashy dash of panache,
the spinning grinning vortex stripped of its values, the
minstrel, the music, the antidote to the boob tube incar-
nate!*

Whew! Cera's certainly got a poetry gene, don't he?

But, McLuhan soon comes to love the floor as
much as he loves the garish mural; in fact, he loves
every square centimetre of the coach house, even more
than he loves Wychwood Park, sometimes, thinks he, if
that's possible.

Guests of the Centre, likely as not, are offered a
cup of tea, a hunk of bread and cheese or, if the situation warrants it, the occasional beer or mug of wine.

Visitors to the Centre note McLuhan's Cambridge
oar, the tan-toned vinyl chaise longue with the lumpy
green mattress, the shadeless floor lamp on the table,
the single chair, the chipped mugs, the lidless teapot,
the single-burner hotplate, and the refrigerator res-
cued from Wells Hill Road.

They also note the beating heart of the Centre in
his element and detect glimmerings of the light that
once burned brightly in his eyes, despite his gaunt
lankiness, despite the thin face with its features loosely
strung together, despite the chronic look of frangible
collapsibility and querulous fatigue.

And, visitors note, most acutely, the frustrations,
the vexations, the rather public displays of anger and

grief for the man he was and now understands he will never be.

With Maurice working alongside Harley as well as the appointment of distinguished authors and English professors Sheila and Wilfred Watson to further aid him in his work at the Centre, McLuhan's anxiously confident he can get up to speed and back in tip-top shape fairly quickly. There are several books with various collaborators in multiple stages of completion. He's as eager to deliver fresh material to his editors and publishers as he is enthusiastic about getting back into the swing of familiar things.

Not entirely without justification, McLuhan variously troubles and terrifies his friends and family. He walks into walls; he forgets where he lives; and, when he's not obsessively twirling his glasses, he's absent-mindedly misplacing them.

His group of assistants, snarkily dubbed "McLuhan's wives," runs interference for the professor until, invariably, their patience runs out, usually after attempting to collaborate with him on one or another of the multi-faceted projects concerning some aspect of McLuhan's famous probes into the nature of most any and everything worthy of attention. McLuhan's intent on revisiting the ways in which technology renders individualism obsolete and makes corporate interdependence mandatory (as well as ways in which the new electronic interdependence recreates the world in the image of a global village, as he initially suggests in *The Gutenberg Galaxy*).

Shortly after the publication of *Counterblast*, a brief collection of his recent essays, Dr. Watson and

McClue tackle the task of pulling together *From Cliché to Archetype* in the fall of 1969.

Under both personal and professional pressures to wrap up the project begun in 1963 (with a contract from Viking Press), the pair determines the book will present an extended dialogue employing techniques reminiscent of the Menippean satirists in at attempt to provide readers with a vivid and comprehensive marshalling of McLuhan's thought. The work will, it is hoped, help to restore the reputation of the world's premier techno-cultural anthropologist as one of the world's equally brilliant literary critics.

As well, McLuhan chuckles, it will take his old rival, Northrop Frye – with his rigid vision and straitjacketed understanding of archetypes – down a peg or two.

McLuhan and Watson begin dictating their book to Margaret Stewart. McLuhan's secretary grows more and more perplexed as days turn into weeks turn into months of wrangling between the two until, inevitably, the dialogue dissolves into a pair of point-counterpoint monologues (a.k.a. analogues).

The bewildered secretary takes notes, first from Watson, then from McLuhan, then from Watson (who contradicts McLuhan), then from McLuhan (who contradicts Watson)...

It falls to Eric to edit and prepare the unusual manuscript from Stewart's notes just in time for the printer to ship finished books in the fall of 1970, the same year another McLuhan volume, *Culture Is Our Business*, reaches retailers.

∞

Relishing the regularly crowded weekly seminar crammed with forty-fifty people (in addition to the dozen students registered in his course) sitting on the floor the evenings it takes place, McLuhan continues his work at the Centre, puffs on his cigars, and is largely unimpressed with the *New Yorker* cartoon asking the question, "Ashley, are you sure it's not too soon to go around parties saying, 'What ever happened to Marshall McLuhan?'"

McLuhan, himself too busy to wonder, has just been appointed a Companion of the Order of Canada and has just received Great Britain's Institute of Public Relations' President's Award, Assumption University's Christian Culture Award plus, despite his feelings of disgust concerning the many failings of Vatican II's Latin-Mass destroyers, he accepts a Vatican appointment as Consultor of the Pontifical Commission for Social Communications, not to mention various honorary degrees and commendations right around the globe.

Equally busy with his civic concerns, McLuhan is working with urban planner and eco-preservationist Jane Jacobs (supported by thousands) protesting the construction of the Spadina Expressway, which will snake straight through the heart of several residential neighbourhoods in Toronto. "Mere concern with efficient traffic flow is a cloacal obsession," opines he, fully aware that "cloacal" means gutter-minded. "Mere concern with efficient traffic flow is a cloacal obsession that sends the city down the drain."

Plans for the expressway are scrapped.

It is at this busy time the McLuhan issue of *Playboy* appears. In the interview, perhaps McLuhan's brightest, the doctor of digitalia's methods, meanings, and essential qualities sparkle with wit and optimism (in startling contrast to the pessimism he's chronically expressing in his own life).

Here, he practises what he preaches, having invested a great deal of energy in one of his pet percepts, the one concerning "putting on" (or wearing or becoming) an audience.

Whether he puts on the *Playboy* interviewer or not in monologues such as the following is certainly not a question easily answered:

"It's inevitable," asserts McLuhan, "that the world-pool of electronic information movement will toss us all about like corks on a stormy sea, but if we keep our cool during the descent into the maelstrom, studying the process as it happens to us and what we can do about it, we can come through…

"I feel that we're standing on the threshold of a liberating and exhilarating world in which the human tribe can become truly one family and man's consciousness can be freed from the shackles of mechanical culture and enabled to roam the cosmos."

Regrettably, at the Centre, the shackles of mechanical culture turn McLuhan into something of a raging bully, most keenly with his assistants, most often with his eldest son, Eric, or his stalwart and trusted friend, electrical-engineer Barrington Nevitt (with whom he's co-authored 1972's *Take Today*, the work he believes will bring together his major themes and most significant insights into the patterns of human and social organization in the global village).

Take Today, virtually ignored by both media and masses, sells little more than four thousand copies; but, *Take Today* underscores his view that all life – mental, material, spiritual, physical – is governed by laws, laws that no one else has even noticed, let alone considered worthy of discussion between the covers of a book.

Take Today is philosophically grounded in this world; it isn't a religious book, but its central idea – issuing from Christ's precepts and McLuhan's understanding of the primary importance of Pentecost in view of the laws he's perceived – the percepts he's unearthed – can provide comfort and enlightenment.

The laws are infallible – as precise as mathematics, as ubiquitous as weather – and, after wrestling with them for almost five decades, he has finally grasped them in all their glory.

Eight years after his father's death, Eric McLuhan's collaboration with him, *Laws of Media: The New Science*, containing both a clarification as well as a clear and concise presentation of what will become the McLuhan Laws of Media – the four laws applying to all media and artefacts – is published. It is – it echoes without saying – McLuhan's Great Book.

Any given medium – be it language, light, DVDs, a chair, or money – demands the following four questions be asked of it:

1. What does the medium extend?
2. What does the medium make obsolete (or cannibalize)?
3. What does the medium retrieve?

4. What does the medium reverse (or into what does the medium flip)?

In this respect, since the McLuhan Laws of Media interact and relate to each other, they are also considered the McLuhan Media Tetrad of extension, obsolescence, retrieval, and reversal. Take, for example, the refrigerator in your kitchen. It preserves and keeps food safe to eat, not to mention making a wide selection of edibles available to all consumers (extension). Although the refrigerator renders the job of the iceman a thing of the past (obsolesence), it also retrieves the individual's ability to share tribally and collectively (among family, friends, congregations, and so on).

It is important to remember, as well, that the McLuhan Tetrad doesn't necessarily mean there is a firm and fast four-part rule which applies to each medium. Like all things McLuhanesque, things are not quite that simple. In other words, as he took pains to explain, the process of the Tetrad is neither sequential, orderly, nor strictly applicable to all four agents in all cases or conditions; rather, the process is simultaneous since all four aspects of the Tetrad already reside in each and every medium and, of necessity, continuously shift both focus and direction.

Still, despite the exciting discoveries, promising projects, and refreshing percepts swirling around his life at the Centre, McLuhan's general irritability is further evidenced in his uncharacteristic disdain for many of his students and, for that matter, anyone who fails to grasp his "percepts" – *Not concepts!* – issuing from his probes in his role as a cultural and technological sleuth or explorer.

More and more, he adopts a whiny-edged attitude laced with surly bitterness and petty contempt, often resorting to the William Empson quote he's carried with him since his Cambridge days to prove his point:

"The only form of response that people in general ever make to something is a numb, somnambulist response. They do whatever happens to come into their heads – like tulips. A tulip does just whatever comes into its head, that's all."

Balancing the low points, of course, are the high points, especially the loyal circle of all-weather friends, fans, and followers who shore him up against the downhill tumble and slide.

Perhaps the highest point of them all during this bleak period occurs when a certain flamboyant politician wishes to repay a certain colourful media advisor for all the great pointers he's freely given him concerning his image this past decade or so.

The night the McLuhans dine at Toronto's Provençal restaurant at the invitation of the prime minister of Canada, the family and the top-secret mystery guest speaker are forty-five minutes late for the weekly seminar, already in high gear without them, thanks largely to the resourcefulness of Eric and Barrington Nevitt.

Eric, knowing where his father is and with whom, keeps the secret to himself until he hears a minor commotion outside the Centre. After he confirms what he believes to be the case is indeed so, he returns to the seminar room:

"Ladies and gentlemen, the Prime Minister of Canada."

The conversation in the room continues. A couple of the participants cast quizzical glances in Eric's direction. Above the din, he again announces the arrival of the prime minister, the special guest speaker at the seminar this evening:

"Ladies and…"

A smiling and dignified gent, signature red rose pinned to his lapel, steps into the room which, after a moment's stunned silence, erupts in a rapture of spontaneous cheers and applause.

"… join me in welcoming the Prime Minister of Canada, Pierre Elliott Trudeau."

∽

The white-haired sage of Wychwood Park and his spunky partner take up yoga together. During their later years, McLuhan especially enjoys breakfast time in their new home, particularly when his wife reads the news from the morning papers to him or takes the time to relay all the details concerning their children's various trials and triumphs, acting as a kind of translator between a father who loves his children but can't quite figure out how to express that love and six children who can't quite figure out how to take their father's disgruntled criticisms, not to mention his overall doom-and-gloominess, as expressions of that love.

On one occasion, Corinne reassures the couple's youngest, Michael, his father does indeed love him (even if his drastic reactions and hippie-hating insults suggest otherwise). On another occasion, she joins with Sheila Watson to calm Michael's older sister, Elizabeth, after their father's dire predictions of widespread violence (directly related to the loss of the identity of the contemporary anybody), racial wars, and mass-murder epidemics to come have scared the wits out of her and reduced her to terrified tears.

On all occasions, McLuhan's wife tactfully and heroically performs the function of family buffer or emotional traffic controller, expertly smoothing things over when her beleaguered and chronically overextended husband hits a particularly rough patch of turbulence with the children everyone knows he deeply loves in his increasingly difficult fashion which, it soon becomes clear, is caused as much by the harrowing surgery he's survived as it is by the ever-deteriorating state of his health.

Initially attributed to exceedingly high blood-pressure levels, the culprit for McLuhan's series of minor heart attacks is eventually discovered: His internal carotid arteries, the major suppliers of fresh blood to the brain, have narrowed dangerously and look to be perilously close to becoming completely blocked at any moment. Tests will need to be done. If the diagnosis proves correct, he will, once again, be forced to endure surgery on his skull.

"Wait a minute! Not so fast!"

Respected neurologist H. J. M. Barnett, flush with excitement, returns with the results of the angiographic test he's just performed on McLuhan at St. Michael's Hospital in downtown Toronto. In the angiography, he explains, he injects dye into the arteries to trace the flow of blood through the patient's brain. He can't believe what this test shows:

"Look at this, see? The internal carotid arteries are indeed blocked, just as we suspected. But, look here: The external carotid artery, the one that supplies blood to the face, scalp, and jaw? That artery has formed huge connecting channels through the base and inside Mac's skull. This kind of thing's normal in some species, say, cats, but it's virtually unheard of in human beings. I've never seen anything like it! I swear! The only thing that compares with this is the carotid-artery system found in tigers! Astonishing, truly astonishing.

"Go home, Tiger, you'll not be needing surgery for this so-called problem."

At home, McLuhan continues his explorations and elaborates upon his theories expounding the nature of new media and their effects on culture and civilization in terms of the dominance of the new acoustic world. According to McLuhan, the global village is populated with "discarnate" human beings who no longer exist as physical presences; instead, the electronic or discarnate person is simply an image or an information pattern, nothing more, thanks to the telephone, computer, television, video camera, etc.

In other words, the very real individual ceases to exist except as a configuration of images or information bits in what he now calls a phantom electronic world. As a result of this split, the discarnate human being, lacking an identity in any real sense, reacts violently.

Violence, as McLuhan observes, is the only recourse for those who have been stripped of their identities, for those who have been rendered discarnate in the new electronic world of acoustic space dominating the global village.

In an age where individuals are reduced to mere images or packets of information, they often resort to violence to overcome their loss of identity and assert their individuality; as a corollary, some of the chief human activities become espionage and surveillance (in everything from police forces, spy satellites, Nielsen ratings, marketing surveys, security guards, focus groups, credit-bureau investigations to social insurance numbers, magnetic-identification strips, prisons, computer cookies, video cameras, and a pair of wise guys forever caught on film):

∞

In Woody Allen's *Annie Hall*, shooting takes place on location in front of the New Yorker Theater at Broadway and 85th Streets. The storyline (the content) involves the director-producer-writer-actor becoming increasingly snarly towards an "academic" behind him in line who's blabbering about McLuhan's ideas.

Allen tells the loudmouth he doesn't know shinnikins from shinola. The loudmouth spouts his credentials and authorities until Allen one-ups him by revealing he happens to have McLuhan with him on hand to disprove the loudmouth's mental macaroni.

Stately – almost magisterially – McLuhan slowly enters scene right in profile view, left side facing the audience. It is in this set of frames, if viewers look very carefully, they will notice McLuhan's three-finger signature good-luck sign which, for him, represents Trinity. (Throughout his life, McLuhan, always the amateur numerologist, considers three and, to a lesser extent, seven, his luckiest numbers. Thirteen is by far the unluckiest of all.)

Nevertheless, it is then in the film that McLuhan tells the pishifying idiot, "You know nothing of my work."

Later, McLuhan explains he'd arrived early; and, until the shooting commenced, he'd had a thorough ball keeping the crowd in stitches laughing along with the ham over his hilarious jokes and head-spinning one-liners (for which he's understandably immortalized).

Then, believe it or not, a hurricane hits. Shooting's postponed. Surprisingly, for reasons beyond McLuhan's ken, Allen vetoes his original (much funnier) line, the one the professor feels best represents him:

"You mean my fallacy is all wrong?"

Near the end of his brilliant and highly controversial career, McLuhan's still diligently at work with one of his final collaborators, Dr. Robert Logan, the highly articulate physicist who introduces the "split-brain hypothesis" to his colleague.

It is the theory that, according to the left-handed McLuhan, vindicates his life's work. To his mind, the right hemisphere of the brain – the home of the acoustic, the simultaneous, and the intuitive – is the hemisphere of the electronic age. Conversely, the left hemisphere – housing the visual, the linear, and the logical – is the hemisphere of the phonetic alphabet and the printing press.

It's a no-brainer McLuhan sees himself as a right-brainer, being the south paw he is (since the right brain controls the left half of the human body and vice versa). Naturally, when McLuhan understands and adopts (or adapts) the neurological implications of the split-brain hypothesis, he further sees another solid example of the schism between visually oriented versus auditory-dominant societies and the shift or break (up, down, and through) accompanying such cultures and civilizations as they develop.

∽

I'm not a crusader, I'm an investigator... The explorer is inconsistent. He must be... I don't prescribe. I merely wish to understand the power of these new forms in order to avoid them!"

∽

In the present era of domination by information, the global village has sloughed off its industrial-age shackles. Now, megabyte millennarians and digital deists trumpet the virtues of the great wired grid, the network consciousness McLuhan envisioned when it was just a techno-gleam in some cyber-geek's eye.

With the hour of radical contingency come round at last, many global villagers, less-than-smitten with the rose-coloured goggle-view of contemporary existence, are justified in adopting a McLuhanesque position when replying to Tom Wolfe's urgent 1967 question – *What if he is right?* – with an urgent question of their own:

Why, in the name of all we hold sacred, wasn't McLuhan wrong?

In his element, McLuhan composes his thoughts while taking
a breather at his beloved Centre, where Cera's
Pied Piper mural is very much a part of the picture.

10

Eloquent Silence

All my work is satire.

– Marshall McLuhan

On 26 September 1979, McLuhan suffers a massive cerebral stroke. The doctors declare he will never walk again. Within two weeks, he's walking. Barely. He is struck with aphasia. His hands are partially paralyzed and he can no longer write or speak (except to say, "oh, boy; oh, boy; oh, boy," "um," "ah," "yes," "uh," and "no," generally punctuated with grimaces, grunts, and shrugs).

He spends long hours in silence resting in an easy chair in the living room at 3 Wychwood Park, close to the fire, rising from time to time to inspect the embers, to recall earlier fires, other flames, brightly burning dreams and desires.

Family, friends, and a steady stream of visitors ease Corinne's burden, taking turns reading everything from the latest academic findings in various fields to popular biographies to portions of James Joyce's *Finnegans Wake* to him:

"By earth and the cloudy but I badly want a brandnew bankside, bedamp and I do, and a plumper at that!"

McLuhan sighs deeply, smiles expansively, and urges his son to continue.

During poignant passages of biographies such as that of the life of Winston Churchill's mother, Jennie, McLuhan breaks right down and bawls, a not-uncommon feature of post-stroke victims (who lose their ability to keep their emotions in check).

In June 1980, the University of Toronto, of the opinion that McLuhan is the Centre for Culture and Technology and the Centre is McLuhan, announces McLuhan's Centre will soon close its doors. The McLuhan Programme in Culture and Technology will replace it, despite howls of outrage issuing from the likes of then-California governor Jerry Brown, Prime Minister Pierre Elliott Trudeau, quipsmith Tom Wolfe, architect Buckminster Fuller and, loudest and proudest of them all, Peter C. Newman, the colourful Editor-in-Chief of *Maclean's* newsmagazine.

∞

"Marsh-Shall, in *Maclean's*, it's Peter Newman! You like him; you love his name, remember? Peter? Saint Peter and the pearly gates and the New Man? Anyway, Peter's writing about the closing of the Centre! Here, here... Look, look at this huge headline, too!

"'Will Our Own Aristotle Be a Prophet Without a Home?'"

"Will he, indeed?! And, right away, he starts, 'McLuhan, one of our few seminal thinkers, is being threatened with eviction.'"

Yes.

"'What's involved is a decision by the University of Toronto, where he has taught since 1946, to shut down McLuhan's world-renowned Centre for Culture and Technology. Although his reputation has endowed the building with an impressive title, the Centre is little more than a converted garage about the size of a modest Victorian stable.'"

Yes.

"'It employs a staff of three and its most prominent decoration is McLuhan's rowing oar from his days at Cambridge. The U of T budgets an annual $75,000 to house its most illustrious professor, but now it has ordered McLuhan to vacate his premises by 30 June 1980.

"'McLuhan, who first came to non-academic prominence in 1959 with his aphorism that "the medium is the message," is currently recovering from a stroke. But his Centre has eight research projects under way and continues to sponsor weekly seminars.'"

Yes!

"'His dozen books, his Schweitzer Fellowship at New York's Fordham University, his countless lectures, and what he likes to describe as his "probes" have turned McLuhan into a contemporary Aristotle. Ironically, the province of Ontario declared him a "natural resource." The term "McLuhanism" was recently listed in *The Oxford English Dictionary*...'"

Oh, boy!

"'Proud we should be, but the University of Toronto's ruling represents all too well the Canadian syndrome of playing down our few resident geniuses. Typically, most of the pressure to restore McLuhan to his ramshackle Centre is coming from Americans, including Buckminster Fuller, Woody Allen, and Tom Wolfe...'"

Oh, yeah!

∞

McLuhan makes his final visit to the doomed Centre accompanied by his loyal secretary, Margaret Stewart.

"It was," Stewart recalls, "a complete garbage dump... All of the records I had made for McLuhan were in a garbage heap. I don't know what happened to all his stuff, but when I saw it I just felt my whole life fall apart.

"I said to Marshall, 'Do you want me to help you?' and he put his arms out and then he came over and he hugged me. It was pitiful. It nearly tore me apart."

The prophet without a home, dazed, shattered, reduced to silent tears, sadly surveys the scene of what can only be described as one incomprehensible crime committed, as it were, on the cusp of closing time.

∞

Sorel Etrog, the highly respected sculptor and long-time family friend, sighs agreeably regarding Marshall McLuhan and his wife, Corinne. He's similarly entranced by the splendid simplicity of the Nativity scene before them as adults and grown children cluster closer together in a warm embrace. It's quiet. It's comforting. It's the season to be jolly in the heart of Toronto where a postcard-perfect winter cityscape is dramatically framed by majestic skyscrapers, the CN Tower, and a blazing sun casting luminous shadows shimmering among cloud-dappled patches of powder-blue sky.

The temperature's brisk but nowhere near bone-chilling; the air magically sparkles with crystalline snow flecks; and, right there, the hushed group of revellers gathers around the holy scene tastefully displayed in the lobby of the Sutton Place Hotel to honour the birth of Christ nineteen-hundred-and-eighty years ago. It's the spirit of the season and the slightly awed, slightly subdued assembly simply basks in the warmth of the shared knowledge this could well be its last evening together.

It's a sobering thought; yet, it fails to dampen the spirits of the McLuhan clan as the huddle links arms to march back up to the sanctuary of Wychwood Park, the family's tiny piece of paradise smack-dab in the centre of Canada's largest city. There, Etrog will join the

McLuhans to celebrate the blessed event by taking his appointed place at the lavishly set dining-room table laden with a feast fit for royal merry-makers.

Etrog joins the McLuhan elders and youngsters respectfully bowing their heads saying grace before the general merriment and joyous festivities begin in earnest. Then, as usual, someone remembers the Christmas when their father was forced to spend the holidays in some back-of-beyond because a severe storm had grounded all planes. Someone else recalls the time one of the youngsters tried to affix the angel to the top of the tree and wound up planting her in a bowl of cranberry sauce instead. Each one dwells fleetingly yet lovingly upon the marvel that Marshall and Corinne McLuhan are still very much in love after forty-odd years in a marriage that has produced six remarkable children following in their parents' ambitious footsteps in several walks of life.

"Well, Marsh," begins Etrog, "I can't remember the last time I saw that satisfied gleam glistening so glowingly in your eyes."

McLuhan grins mischievously, acknowledges Etrog's alliterative tribute gracefully, and emphatically nods his head.

"You do look happy, Marsh-Shall," adds his wife, "happy in a contented and pleased way. Am I right?"

"Oh, yeah!"

Etrog, in high spirits himself, toasts the McLuhans and makes a bit of a joke about how the greatest communications theorist the world's ever known can do little but radiate spontaneous joy, a not unkindly remark considering the media maestro's recently returned home from his sojourn in the hospital following the stroke that's silenced his compelling voice.

McLuhan loves the idea of spontaneous joy. He smiles almost beatifically, holding his arms aloft as if to say, Who needs to talk when all of THIS is happening – who could get an edge in word-wise, anyways?

The crew dissolves in giggle fits.

"Dad's always been a card, eh?"

"Yes," his wife admits, "but a loveable one, a wonderfully loveable card – an ace, in fact."

∽

Less than a week later, the last of the McLuhans' visitors, Frank Stroud, a Jesuit priest from New York, spends New Year's Eve celebrating with the ace and his family.

"Frank? You see that pin on Marsh's lapel? Guess what it is!"

"Oh, Corinne, I'm an American, but even I don't have to guess," replies Stroud, "it's Marshall's Companion of the Order of Canada pin. I noticed it earlier this evening when I was saying Mass. I must say, it looks very good on him. And your country."

"Does, doesn't it? Funny thing about that little pin. That little 'trinket' means more to Marshall than any other single thing he's ever accomplished or achieved. It means the world to you, doesn't it, Marsh?"

"Oh, yeah," McLuhan responds quietly, "oh, yeah." He shyly bows his head to conceal the sudden flow of tears and then, just as suddenly, he raises his eyes to scrutinize the features of his wife, children, grandchildren, and Father Stroud, almost as if he's somehow aware he's seeing them one final time.

The tears fall freely as Corinne explains gently, "everything's okay. *Really.* These are just tears of joy. Right, Marsh-Shall?"

"Oh, yeah!"

Later that New Year's Eve, Canada's Aristotle mounts the stairs to the master bedroom of the McLuhans' cherished Wychwood home for the last time, striking out for new territory in the land of dreamless sleep, safe in the arms of his Creator at last.

Count on it.

McLuhan in a moment of spontaneous joy.

Chronology of
Marshall McLuhan
(1911-1980)

Compiled by Judith Fitzgerald

MCLUHAN AND HIS TIMES	CANADA AND THE WORLD
1846	**1846**
William McLuhan Jr of County Down, Ireland arrives in Canada. Accompanying him is his son, James Hilliard McLuhan, grandfather of Marshall McLuhan.	Richard March Hoe invents the rotary printing press. This machine, which prints 8,000 sheets an hour, is the forerunner of the modern printing press.
	1852
	The first underwater communications cable in North America is installed between Cape Tormentine, New Brunswick and Carleton Head, Prince Edward Island.
	1858
	A telegraphic message is transmitted from North America to Britain for the first time.

McLUHAN AND HIS TIMES	CANADA AND THE WORLD
	1867 Ontario, Quebec, Nova Scotia, and New Brunswick confederate, creating the Dominion of Canada. Manitoba follows in 1870, British Columbia in 1871, Prince Edward Island in 1873, Saskatchewan and Alberta in 1905, and Newfoundland in 1949.
	1872 To encourage prairie settlement, the federal government passes the Dominion Lands Act. A ten-dollar registration fee gives applicants clear titles to their own 160-acre quarter section of land once they prove they are there to stay.
1874 James McLuhan marries Margaret Grieve, who had emigrated with her parents from Scotland when she was a child. Their second son, Herbert Ernest McLuhan, is Marshall McLuhan's father.	**1874** Toronto student Henry Woodward patents the first incandescent lamp with an electric light bulb. A share in the patent is sold to Thomas Edison (who delivers his new and improved version to the world in 1879). In Brantford, Ontario, Alexander Graham Bell conceives of the telephone while experimenting with improvements on the telegraph system.
	1875 The Supreme Court of Canada is established.

McLuhan and His Times	Canada and the World
	1877 Electricity is used for lighting for the first time in Canada (on Montreal's waterfront).
	1879 At a lecture in Toronto, Ontario, Sir Sandford Fleming proposes that the world be divided into twenty-four equal time zones.
	1880 Britain transfers jurisdiction over Arctic islands to Canada.
	1885 The transcontinental Canadian Pacific Railway (CPR) is completed, joining Canada's east and west coasts by telegraph as well as rail.
	The North-West Rebellion breaks out. Louis Riel leads the Métis in protest against Ottawa's handling of Métis land claims. Riel is hanged for treason in November.
1889 McLuhan's mother, Elsie Naomi Hall, daughter of Henry Selden Hall and Margaret Marshall, is born in Nova Scotia's Annapolis Valley.	**1889** The CPR telegraph line is linked with the transatlantic telegraph cable.
	Anson McKim opens Canada's first advertising agency in Montreal.
	1900 Quebec-born inventor Reginald Aubrey Fessenden discovers the superheterodyne principle, the

McLuhan and His Times	Canada and the World
	foundation of modern broadcasting.
	1901
	In St. John's, Newfoundland, Guglielmo Marconi is on the receiving end of the first wireless message ever transmitted across the Atlantic from England.
	1906
	Reginald Aubrey Fessenden invents wireless voice transmission.
1907	
James McLuhan, at seventy, moves his family from Ontario to Alberta.	
1908	**1908**
Elsie Hall joins her parents, who had moved to western Canada two years earlier. She teaches school in Creighton, Alberta and lodges with the family of James McLuhan.	In the U.S., Henry Ford introduces the Model T.
1909	**1909**
Herbert McLuhan and Elsie Hall marry in the Hall family home in Minburn, Alberta.	Bakelite, the first totally synthetic plastic, is invented.
1911	**1911**
Herbert and Elsie McLuhan's first child, Herbert Marshall McLuhan, is born in Edmonton, Alberta. His brother, Maurice Raymond, is born two years later.	Robert Borden leads the Conservatives to a Canadian federal-election win.
	Carl Jung founds Analytic Psychology and develops the notion of the collective unconscious.

MCLUHAN AND HIS TIMES

1914
Herbert McLuhan loses everything when a real-estate boom in Edmonton goes bust. Two years later the family settles in Winnipeg, Manitoba.

CANADA AND THE WORLD

1914
The First World War begins, touched off by the assassination of Austria-Hungary's heir to the throne, Archduke Ferdinand, in Sarajevo on June 28 by a Serbian nationalist. Canada, as part of the British Empire, sends 625,000 men and several thousand women to war between 1914 and 1918.

1917
In Canada, artist Tom Thomson drowns in Algonquin Park.

At the Battle of Vimy Ridge in April, Canadian soldiers fight as a unit for the first time and achieve victory where the British and French have failed.

Wartime strains bring about the collapse of the Czarist regime in Russia. Lenin returns from exile in Switzerland. The Bolsheviks seize power in the Russian Revolution.

1918
The First World War ends. Fighting stops at 11:00 AM on 11 November 1918. Ten million Europeans alone have died on the battlefield. The wounded number at least 21 million. One in ten Canadians who fought on the European battlefields has died. As many return wounded.

1919
The Winnipeg General Strike, involving about 30,000 workers,

Marshall McLuhan

culminates in 21 June's "Bloody Saturday" in which the Mounties kill two men and wound many others. The general strike collapses several days later.

Canada joins the League of Nations.

Sir Wilfrid Laurier dies.

The first radio broadcast offered on a regular basis make its debut in Canada, at station XWA in downtown Montreal. XWA's transmitter, set up by the Marconi Wireless Telegraph Company of Canada, is utilized by CFCF – one of the earliest stations in the world to feature regular programming.

1920
The Group of Seven is founded by Frank Carmichael, Lawren Harris, A. Y. Jackson, Franz Johnston, Arthur Lismer, J. E. H. Mac-Donald, and F. H. Varley.

In the U.S., KDKA, a Pittsburgh Westinghouse station, transmits the first commercial radio broadcast.

1921
After numerous moves, Herbert and Elsie McLuhan take up residence in Fort Rouge, a Scots and Irish district of Winnipeg.

1921
William Lyon Mackenzie King brings the Liberals to power in Ottawa; Agnes MacPhail becomes the first woman to win a seat in a federal election.

McLuhan and His Times

Canada and the World

Sir William Stephenson conceives of a novel method of wireless transmission of photographs. His discovery, used by newspapers everywhere, contributes to the development of television (which transmits images in somewhat the same fashion).

1922
Elsie McLuhan begins touring Manitoba as an elocutionist and monologist.

1923
The discovery of insulin, for the treatment of diabetes, earns Canadian Frederick Banting the Nobel Prize for physiology. He shares half the prize money with co-researcher Charles Henry Best.

1925
The invention of the world's first alternating-current radio tube, by Toronto-born Edward Samuel Rogers, allows radios to utilize household electricity.

1927
A show of West Coast art in Ottawa exhibits the paintings of Emily Carr.

1928
McLuhan enters the University of Manitoba, the third largest university in Canada. Among the subjects he studies in his first two years are English, Latin, history, economics, psychology, astronomy, and geology.

1928
In the U.S., colour television is demonstrated for the first time by inventor J. L. Baird.

Canada boasts sixty-plus licensed radio stations.

McLUHAN AND HIS TIMES

CANADA AND THE WORLD

1929
Around the world, stock markets crash on 29 October, ushering in the Great Depression (the effects of which are felt for a decade). Canada, as a major exporter of raw materials, is particularly devastated when global overproduction drives prices down dramatically. Imports and exports tumble.

1930
McLuhan's first published article, "Macauley – What a Man!" appears in the university's student paper, *The Manitoban.*

1930
Under R. B. Bennett, the Conservatives come to power.

In the U.S., Philo T. Farnsworth develops the cathode ray tube.

The first large-scale analogue computer is built by Vannevar Bush at the Massachusetts Institute of Technology (MIT).

1931
Canada's independence from Britain is recognized with the Statute of Westminster.

1932
McLuhan travels to England accompanied by fellow student Tom Easterbrook. The pair work as crewmen on a cattle boat. McLuhan falls in love (with medical student Marjorie Norris). He also discovers G. K. Chesterton's *What's Wrong with the World?*

1932
More than 1,500,000 Canadians are dependent upon relief after industrial production in Canada falls by half between 1929 and 1932; the Co-operative Commonwealth Federation party (CCF), founded at Calgary, Alberta, advocates social and economic reforms.

1933
After obtaining his B.A., McLuhan begins work on "George Meredith

1933
Canadian unemployment peaks at 20 per cent.

McLUHAN AND HIS TIMES	CANADA AND THE WORLD
as a Poet and Dramatic Novelist," his master's thesis.	In France, physicists Frederick and Irene Joliot-Curie discover that radioactive elements can be prepared from stable elements.
	In Germany, Hitler is named Chancellor.
1934 The University of Manitoba accepts McLuhan's master's thesis. He begins two years at Cambridge University's Trinity Hall.	**1934** The world's first surviving quintuplets, the Dionne daughters, are born near North Bay, Ontario.
1935 McLuhan meets F. R. Leavis and G. K. Chesterton; his thinking is additionally influenced by I. A. Richards and Mansfield Forbes.	**1935** The On-To-Ottawa Trek of unemployed workers culminates with the Regina Riot after Prime Minister R. B. Bennett orders a halt to the trek.
	The Bank of Canada begins operations.
	Prime Minister Bennett introduces his "New Deal" but is defeated in a general election by Mackenzie King and the Liberals.
1936 Leaving Cambridge, McLuhan lands a job teaching in the English department of the University of Wisconsin.	**1936** The Canadian Broadcasting Corporation (CBC) is established by the Liberal government with a mandate to develop a domestic radio network with Canadian content in English and French.
	Maurice Duplessis and the Union Nationale come to power in Quebec.

McLuhan and His Times

1937
St. Louis University, reputed to be the finest Catholic university in America, hires McLuhan to teach in its English Department. McLuhan converts to Catholicism.

1939
McLuhan and Corinne Keller Lewis marry at St. Louis Cathedral on the campus of St. Louis University. Mr. and Mrs. McLuhan honeymoon in Italy and France. The newlyweds settle in Cambridge just as the Second World War breaks out. McLuhan chooses Thomas Nashe as the subject of his dissertation.

1940
McLuhan and his wife board different ships to leave England. McLuhan, the citizen of a country at war, sails from Liverpool to Montreal. Corinne, as the citizen of a non-belligerent country, the United States, sails from Ireland to New York. The couple returns to St. Louis where McLuhan resumes his duties at Saint Louis University as well as continuing to work on his Ph.D dissertation. He makes his debut on radio with a ten-minute talk.

Canada and the World

1937
The forerunner of Air Canada – Trans-Canada Air Lines – is founded as a subsidiary of the Canadian National Railway (CNR).

1939
The Second World War breaks out shortly after Nazi Germany invades Poland on 1 September. Two days later, Britain and France declare war on Germany. Canada declares war; close to a million Canadians see military service overseas and in Canada. At least 40,000 are killed.

King George VI and Queen Elizabeth are enthusiastically welcomed during their tour of Canada.

1940
The government of Canada undertakes an unemployment insurance scheme.

1941
The Canadian Women's Army Corps is established.

McLuhan and His Times

1942
Marshall and Corinne McLuhan's first child, Thomas Eric Marshall McLuhan, is born on 19 January.

1943
The St. Louis draft board classifies McLuhan 1-A. Directing a play in Detroit, Elsie alerts her son to the presence of Wyndham Lewis in Windsor, Ontario. Lewis is an influential painter and novelist whose theory that media extend the human body will influence McLuhan's own theories on media a great deal. McLuhan's dissertation is approved by Cambridge.

1944
McLuhan accepts a job as head of the English department at Assumption College, a small Catholic institution in Windsor.

1945
On 26 October, Corinne gives birth to twin daughters, Teresa Carolyn and Mary Corinne.

Canada and the World

1942
A plebiscite on conscription is held; the expulsion of Japanese from Canada's Pacific coast begins.

Italian-born U.S. physicist Enrico Fermi produces the first controlled nuclear chain reaction.

1943
The first nuclear reactor begins operating.

1944
Canada participates in the Normandy invasion.

The first socialist government in North America is formed in Saskatchewan by the CCF.

The Family Allowance Act, Canada's first universal social-welfare programme, is passed by Prime Minister Mackenzie King's government and comes into effect.

1945
The Second World War ends, having claimed the lives of 60 million people, many civilians among them. Germany surrenders in May. The

McLuhan and His Times

Canada and the World

U.S. drops atomic bombs on Japan on 6 August (Hiroshima) and 9 August (Nagasaki); Japan surrenders on 2 September.

Canada joins the United Nations.

Vannevar Bush conceives of the Memex, a hypothetical machine that finds information through associative links rather than indexing (which lays the theoretical groundwork for hypertext and the World Wide Web).

1946

McLuhan receives an offer to teach at the University of Toronto's St. Michael's College. He is one of the two faculty members who are not priests.

1946

Parliament adopts an act creating a separate Canadian citizenship (distinct from British citizenship).

The concept of the fully automated factory is developed by Canadian Eric W. Leaver. His Automatic Machine Control by Recorded Operation system breaks new ground in technology.

1947

McLuhan is promoted to full professor at the University of Toronto (U of T).

The McLuhans' third daughter, Stephanie Lewis, is born 14 October.

1947

In the U.S., the sound barrier is broken for the first time with an experimental rocket.

British physicist Dennis Gabor develops the principles of holography.

The Polaroid camera is developed.

1948

McLuhan, in the company of Hugh Kenner, visits Ezra Pound at

1948

Louis St. Laurent succeeds W. L. M. King and terminates King's

McLUHAN AND HIS TIMES

St. Elizabeth's Hospital for the Criminally Insane in Washington, DC. McLuhan's preoccupation with the Symbolist poets increases.

1950
Elizabeth Anne, the McLuhans' fourth daughter, is born on 2 August. McLuhan meets Ted Carpenter from the U of T Department of Anthropology, a friend for life.

1951
The Mechanical Bride, representing McLuhan's social criticism of the 1940s, is published by Vanguard Press. In a letter to Ezra Pound, McLuhan refers to himself as an "intellectual thug." When McLuhan begins his sixth year of teaching at U of T, he moves his family to 81 St. Mary's Street on the campus of St. Michael's.

CANADA AND THE WORLD

twenty-two years as Canada's Prime Minister.

1949
Canada joins the North Atlantic Treaty Organization (NATO). Newfoundland joins Confederation.

1950
The C-102 "Jetliner" aircraft makes the first jet transport flight in North America, flying from Toronto to New York in seventy-five minutes and carrying the first jet airmail. Built by Avro of Toronto, the aircraft was designed in Canada but never produced commercially.

The Korean War breaks out after North Korea invades South Korea. Twenty-two thousand Canadians serve.

1951
The census for this year reveals that half of Canada's families, particularly in rural areas, do not yet own electric refrigerators or vacuum cleaners. Sixty per cent have no car and 40 per cent lack a telephone. One in three dwellings has yet to acquire hot and cold running water.

The National Ballet of Canada is established.

Marshall McLuhan

MCLUHAN AND HIS TIMES

1952
Michael Charles, the McLuhan's second son and last child, is born on 19 October.

1953
The Ford Foundation bestows a grant worth $44,250 upon the University of Toronto's Marshall McLuhan and Ted Carpenter. It allows the duo to set up an interdepartmental seminar in culture and communications. Their journal, *Explorations*, which raises the profile of the seminar, is also made possible by the grant.

1955
McLuhan is invited to speak at a communications seminar at Columbia University, his first significant presentation to an American audience. The McLuhans form "Idea Consultants" with friends in an effort to sell creative ideas to businesses. Not a single idea is sold, and the company closes within two years.

CANADA AND THE WORLD

1952
Beginning in Toronto and Montreal, television broadcasting spreads quickly to other Canadian cities. Canadians buy television sets (with the standard-issue ten-inch black-and-white screen) en masse. *Hockey Night in Canada* becomes the centrepiece of Saturday nights for many.

1953
Ontario's Shakespearean Festival opens in Stratford.

The Korean War ends.

1954
Construction begins on the St. Lawrence Seaway.

1955
Across the Arctic coast, from Alaska to Greenland, Distant Early Warning (DEW) stations are built as part of North America's defences against the Soviet Union.

McLuhan and His Times

1956
The McLuhans buy their first home, a comfortable dwelling located at 29 Wells Hill Road, a short distance from the campus of the University of Toronto in the city's Annex neighbourhood.

1957
McLuhan utters his famous pronouncement, "The medium is the message," for the first time at a conference for radio broadcasters.

Canada and the World

1956
American computer scientist John McCarthy coins the term "Artificial Intelligence" (AI).

The first transatlantic telephone cable is installed.

1957
The federal Progressive Conservatives are elected under John G. Diefenbaker (who replaces Prime Minister Louis St. Laurent).

Lester B. Pearson wins the Nobel Peace Prize.

The Canada Council is founded in support of culture and the arts.

The North American Air Defence Command (NORAD) comes into being, integrating certain portions of the Canadian and American Air Forces.

The U.S.S.R. launches Sputnik 1, the world's first artificial satellite.

1958
The advanced jet interceptor Avro Arrow CF-105, designed to defend Canada's North from Soviet bombers, makes its debut.

A coal-mining disaster at Springhill, Nova Scotia claims the lives of seventy-four underground workers.

McLuhan and His Times

1959

A proposal submitted by McLuhan to design a teaching method on the effects of media is approved by the National Association of Educational Broadcasters (NAEB) in the United States.

The journal *Explorations* ceases publication.

Canada and the World

1959

Completion of the St. Lawrence Seaway links the Great Lakes and the Atlantic Ocean by means of the St. Lawrence River.

Prime Minister Diefenbaker cancels the Avro Arrow programme. (All six aircraft that had been produced are destroyed.)

The U.S. army successfully sends monkeys 500 kilometres into space.

Introduction of second-generation (completely transistorized) computers.

The Dalai Lama is exiled from Tibet.

1960

Canada's government announces the country's contribution of $25 million towards the construction of the longest submarine telephone cable in the world. The Commonwealth Transpacific Cable is to stretch from Sydney, Australia to Bamfield, British Columbia via Norfolk Island, Fiji, and the Hawaiian Islands.

Quebec's new Liberal government institutes measures that eventually come to be described as the "Quiet Revolution."

MCLUHAN AND HIS TIMES	CANADA AND THE WORLD
	Status Indians (governed by the Federal Indian Act) are granted the vote in federal elections.
	In the U.S., John Fitzgerald Kennedy is elected president. He is the 35th president and the first Roman Catholic to hold this office.
	1961 The New Democratic Party (NDP) is launched. Tommy Douglas is chosen as leader.
1962 *The Gutenberg Galaxy* is published; it earns McLuhan the Governor General's Award for Critical Prose.	**1962** Saskatchewan introduces Medicare.
	The Cuban Missile Crisis brings the U.S. and U.S.S.R. to the brink of war.
	"Telstar," the world's first telecommunications satellite, is launched into orbit. Satellites make worldwide communication networks possible.
1963 To bring together academics and researchers to analyze the effects of technology on culture, McLuhan launches the Centre for Culture and Technology at the University of Toronto.	**1963** The Liberals are elected to federal office under Lester B. Pearson.
	In the U.S., race riots and freedom marches inflame the country; the government sends troops into Vietnam; President Kennedy is assassinated.
1964 McGraw-Hill publishes *Understanding Media: The Extensions of*	**1964** The Beatles appear on the Ed Sullivan show.

McLUHAN AND HIS TIMES

Man, an examination of the nature and permutations of many media.

1965
California "genius scouts" Gerald Feigen and Howard Gossage "discover" McLuhan.

1966
Enamoured of McLuhan, *Newsweek*, *The New York Times*, *Life*, *Fortune*, and *Esquire* profile him and his ideas in depth over the next two years. During this period, McLuhan produces articles for (or provides interviews to) *Look*, *TV Guide*, *McCalls*, *Glamour*, *Vogue*, *Family Circle*, *Mademoiselle* and, later still, to *Playboy*, *The Saturday Evening Post*, and *Harper's Bazaar*.

1967
In January, the New York State Board of Regents approves McLuhan's nomination to the Albert Schweitzer Chair in the Humanities at Fordham Univer-

CANADA AND THE WORLD

The first fully automated factory, the Sara-Lee food processing plant, opens using computer-operated equipment.

1965
Canada's new Maple Leaf flag replaces the Red Ensign.

The Auto Pact, an agreement between Canada and the United States, brings free trade to the automobile industry. Canada's auto industry thrives as a result.

Publication of George Grant's *Lament for a Nation*.

American students protest the war in Vietnam.

1966
British engineers show that data in the form of light beams can be transmitted over long distances in glass fibres. This discovery will lead to the development of fibre-optic cables.

1967
Canada celebrates its centennial. *Expo 67: Man and His World* is held on an island in the St. Lawrence River at Montreal. It draws the participation of sixty countries

McLUHAN AND HIS TIMES

sity. A grant of $100,000 accompanies the appointment. *The Medium Is The Massage* is published. The McLuhans move to New York City. McLuhan addresses IBM, AT&T, the American Marketing Association, and the Container Corporation of America as well as the National Bureau of Standards and the International Symposium on Technology and World Trade. NBC airs a segment entitled *This Is Marshall McLuhan* in its Experiment-in-TV series. On 25 November McLuhan undergoes surgery to remove a life-threatening meningioma at New York's Columbia-Presbyterian Hospital. The procedure becomes the longest neurosurgical operation in American medical history.

CANADA AND THE WORLD

and the attention of fifty million visitors.

In the U.S., 50,000 people demonstrate in Washington D.C. against the Vietnam War.

1968
The McLuhans move to 3 Wychwood Park in Toronto after twelve years on Wells Hill Road. McLuhan resumes his Fordham teaching commitments and, by February, his speaking engagements. *War and Peace in the Global Village* is published by Bantam Books. *Through the Vanishing Point: Space in Poetry and Painting* is also published, but it garners scant attention.

1968
Under Pierre Elliott Trudeau, the Liberals win the federal election.

In the U.S., civil rights leader Martin Luther King and presidential candidate Robert Kennedy are assassinated.

1969
Counterblast is published by Harcourt, Brace, and World.

1969
Canada's Parliament adopts the Official Languages Bill, creating greater linguistic equality between anglophones and francophones.

McLUHAN AND HIS TIMES	CANADA AND THE WORLD
	ARPANet, the Internet's predecessor, is born when computers at UCLA, Stanford, Santa Barbara, and Utah are linked.
	American astronaut Neil Armstrong is the first man to walk on the moon. The event is televised worldwide to 100 million viewers.
1970 McLuhan travels extensively to numerous speaking engagements. *Culture Is Our Business* is published by McGraw-Hill, while *From Cliché to Archetype* is published by Viking Press.	**1970** "The October Crisis" occurs in Quebec. The War Measures Act is invoked.
1971 Anticoagulants are used to treat a blockage in McLuhan's right internal carotid artery.	**1971** The government of Canada adopts a policy of multiculturalism.
1972 McLuhan makes more than thirty appearances on TV or in person. *Take Today* is published.	**1972** The establishment of the world's first domestic communications satellite system is accomplished with the launch of Canada's Anik-1 satellite from Cape Canaveral. Team Canada defeats the Soviet hockey team in a series that attracts huge Canadian television audiences. Joey Smallwood resigns as Newfoundland's premier.

MCLUHAN AND HIS TIMES

1973
McLuhan has collected eight honorary doctorates.

1974
McLuhan's speaking engagements take him to Sweden, Mexico, Greece, and several North American cities, Toronto, San Francisco, Charlottetown, Philadelphia, and Montreal among them.

1975
McLuhan appears on BBC TV, gives the Gerstein Lecture Series at Toronto's York University, and speaks to SRO (standing room only) audiences in the Bahamas, Spain, and Switzerland as well as numerous U.S. cities including St. Louis, Atlanta, New York, and Dallas.

1976
Filmmaker Woody Allen requests that McLuhan play himself in a cameo role in *Annie Hall*. McLuhan spends two weeks in hospital after a mild heart attack. His rapid recovery encourages him to begin accepting speaking engagements for 1977.

1977
City as Classroom, the last McLuhan book to appear in his lifetime, is published.

1978
McLuhan briefly immerses himself in the works of Derrida, Foucault, and Ricoeur before

CANADA AND THE WORLD

1974
French becomes Quebec's official language as its National Assembly adopts Bill-22 forwarded by Robert Bourassa's government.

1976
A Parti Québécois government is elected in Quebec.

Montreal hosts the Olympic Games.

discarding the basic premises of both structuralism and post-structuralism.

1979
McLuhan's final academic year begins, while 30 June 1980 is set as his last day on the payroll. On 26 September, McLuhan suffers a massive stroke. Ten days after entering St. Michael's Hospital, he undergoes surgery. The stroke spares his bodily functions but, in a cruel irony, he is afflicted with aphasia and cannot speak.

1980
The University of Toronto announces that the Centre for Culture and Technology will close on 30 June. Corinne throws a party for her husband's sixty-ninth birthday on 21 July. The couple celebrates forty-one years of marriage. Sometime during the night of 31 December, McLuhan dies peacefully in his sleep.

1979
The Progressive Conservatives under Joe Clark win the federal election.

Quebec's James Bay hydroelectric project produces its first electricity.

1980
The majority of Quebeckers vote *non* in a referendum that seeks a mandate for the Parti Québécois to negotiate sovereignty association with the rest of Canada.

2001
Internet architects, pressed by a shortage of Internet Protocol addresses caused by the immense proliferation of electronic devices, propose a new addressing system that will accommodate 340,282, 366,920,938,463,463,374,607,431, 768,211,456 addresses.

Sources Consulted

BERCUSON, David J. and J. L. GRANATSTEIN. *The Collins Dictionary of Canadian History: 1867 to the Present*. Toronto: Collins, 1988.

FINKEL, Alvin. *Our Lives: Canada after 1945*. Toronto: James Lorimer and Company Ltd., Publisher, 1997.

FRANCIS, Douglas R., Richard JONES, and Donald B. SMITH. *Destinies: Canadian History Since Confederation*. Toronto: Harcourt Brace & Company Canada Ltd., 1996.

GORDON, W. Terrence. *Marshall McLuhan: Escape into Understanding*. Toronto: Stoddart, 1997.

MARCHAND, Philip. *Marshall McLuhan: The Medium and the Messenger*. Toronto: Random House, 1989.

MCLUHAN, Eric and Frank ZINGRONE. *Essential McLuhan*. Concord: Anansi, 1995.

MCLUHAN, Marshall. *Counterblast*. Toronto: McClelland and Stewart, 1969.

———. *Culture Is Our Business*. New York: McGraw-Hill, 1970.

———. With Wilfred Watson. *From Cliché to Archetype*. New York: Viking, 1970.

————. *The Gutenberg Galaxy: The Making of Typographic Man*. Toronto: University of Toronto Press, 1962.

————. With Quentin Fiore and Jerome Agel. *The Medium Is the Massage: An Inventory of Effects*. New York: Bantam, 1967.

————. *Understanding Media: The Extensions of Man*. New York: McGraw-Hill, 1964.

MOLINARO, Matie, William TOYE, and Corinne MCLUHAN , ed. *Letters of Marshall McLuhan*. Toronto: Oxford University Press, 1987.

NADER, Ralph, Nadia MILLERON, and Duff CONACHER. *Canada Firsts*. Toronto: McClelland and Stewart Inc., 1992.

NEVITT, Barrington with Maurice McLuhan. (Editors: Frank Zingrone, Wayne Constantineau, Eric McLuhan.) *Who Was Marshall McLuhan?: Exploring a Mosaic of Impressions*. Toronto: Stoddart, 1995.

NEWMAN, Peter C. "Will Our Own 'Aristotle' Be a Prophet Without a Home?" *Maclean's* (17 March 1980).

SAYWELL, John. *Canada: Pathways to the Present*. Toronto: Stoddart, 1999.

Index